Knitly
Joined
Together

Knitly
Joined
Together

By Jacob Luffy

PINECREST PUBLICATIONS
Salisbury Center, NY 13454

First Edition
First Printing, August 1997

Copyright © 1997
Jacob Luffy

ISBN 0-9639416-4-X

Printed by
Pinecrest Publications
PO Box 320
Salisbury Center, NY 13454-0320

Table of Contents

Dedication... vii

Forward ix

Introduction xiii

Chapter One
No Other Foundation................................ 17

Chapter Two
Are Ye Not Yet Carnal? 27

Chapter Three
The Judgment Seat Of Christ: NOW! 43

Chapter Four
The Righteousness Of The Law Fulfilled 59

Chapter Five
Biblical Prosperity................................... 75

Chapter Six
The True Worshippers Of God 87

Chapter Seven
Let Us Keep The Feast............................... 101

Chapter Eight
Appreciation Of The Body Of Christ 117

Chapter Nine
The Local Body — Corinthian Or Antiochian 127

Conclusion... 139

About The Title

The word "Knitly" has been coined by the author to reinforce the central truth of the book. According to Websters, the word "joined" means "to attach," or "to connect physically." The word "knit," however, implies a stronger union whereby the two or more become one as in the "knitting" of bones together.

It is in this sense, the Lord would join and knit His body together. The truths and principles found in this book will help all those who desire to grow into the fulness and stature of Christ and who desire to supply to the body that which the call of God has ordained for them individually. Church splits and divisions and strife are eliminated when believers are rooted and grounded in the love and truth of God. If you have hungered for spiritual maturity, for unity in the fellowship you attend, and for the personal knowledge of God, "Knitly Joined Together" will satisfy your heart, and assembling yourself together with other believers will never be the same again.

Dedication

Over the past years, many members of the Body of Christ have added to my spiritual welfare. Some of these contributions have been invaluable. To those who made them, I am ever grateful. There is one member in particular, whose ministry has been deeply and abundantly imprinted upon my heart. His is a ministry of the Spirit and not of the letter, written upon the fleshly tables of believers' hearts.

Many of the saints of the churches which Paul began, carried a great love in their heart for this apostle who sacrificed so much on their behalf. They no doubt counted it an honor that God would lavish such a man upon them.

So too, I consider it my great privilege to have had a man of such richness minister to me. This book will no doubt reflect much of what he has taught me. My life has, time and again, been enriched and changed through his life being surrendered to our Lord. He has truly been an "effectual worker" for my spiritual benefit, and according to the testimonies of so many others, theirs as well. It is therefore with great appreciation and eternal indebtedness that I dedicate this book to my teacher and friend, Charles A. Haun.

The greatest truth I have learned through all of my afflictions is that I am very dependent upon the other members of the Body of Christ. We need one another. No one can afford to despise the least of the brethren. It is because of some of you that the Lord has sustained me. There has come to my heart a much greater appreciation and sense of need for my brothers and sisters in Jesus. I cannot sufficiently express my gratefulness to you all.

We would all do well to come to a new awareness of our need for one another. It is about time that the members of the Body of Christ come to be dedicated to one another as much as each is dedicated to his own well being. It is time for us to fulfill the Scriptural exhortations concerning our relationships to one another. It has been easy for many brethren to fulfill the prophecy of Jesus in Matthew 24:10: "And then shall many be offended, and shall betray one another, and shall hate one another." It is time to repent and change. Let us begin to fulfill the positive exhortations:

John 13:34, "A new commandment I give unto you, That ye love one another; as I have loved you, that ye also love one another."

In His Resurrection Life.

Charles Haun

Charles Haun

Forward

Dear reader, consider the words of this book with an open heart towards God for they are bread to him who hungers for God, and seed to the one who desires to feed those who have a like hunger. Jacob Luffy deals with the mystery that has been hidden in the heart of God the Father from eternity past unto this present time. This mystery is the union God desires to have with his people and their subsequent union with one another.

These words do not just come from the author's mind or mouth, but also from his life; a life that has tasted of the good word of God and found it to be "honey from the rock," tested, tried and true. God's word never returns void when it is received and applied in one's life. So too, the truths found in this book, which have somehow been neglected by this present generation of Christians, will now bring restoration to them, as they endeavor to bring healing to the nations.

The church must not forget that for God to use us to restore and bring health to others, we must first be healthy ourselves. The author so aptly brings this truth into focus, yet all the while centering on, "Christ in us, our hope of (that) glory."

The depth of the word contained herein will not be obtained in a single reading. Rather you will want to use this book as a study text to refer to again and again. Pastors, teachers, and church leaders will find much help and direction as they endeavour to bring their flocks into the unity and the maturity that God desires for his people. The attainment of the fulness of the stature of Christ is the purpose of all ministry. Only when this maturity occurs in the church, will the world see Christ as God the Father intends.

As you read these pages, may the Lord Jesus work in your hearts the qualities of His bride, "A glorious church without spot or wrinkle, washed in the blood of the Lamb." And as you become one with Him, you will join in the cry of the Spirit, "Come!" And let him who heareth say "come!" And let him who is athirst come." And whosoever will, let him take of the water of life freely."(Revelation 22:17) For it is in giving the Lord Jesus Christ his rightful place in our hearts that we will be "Knitly Joined Together" now and throughout the ages to come.

Philip J. Palutro

"That their hearts might be comforted, being knit together in love, and unto all riches of the full assurance of understanding, to the acknowledgement of the mystery of God, and of the Father, and of Christ; In whom are hid all the treasures of wisdom and knowledge."
Colossians 2:2-3 (KJV)

Introduction

"That in all things He might have the preeminence" (Col. 1:18).

The unity of the Spirit in the Body of Christ results from each individual believer being correctly related to the Head. When Jesus is given the preeminence in our hearts, edification of the Body will always result. From him the whole body, joined and held together by every supporting ligament, grows and builds itself up in love, as each part does its work (Eph. 4:16, NIV). As we hold the Head, we are directed in the work the Lord would have us do, and we are enabled by Him to do that work. It is, however, a common occurrence that preeminence is given to someone or something else in any particular group of believers.

Every local assembly of believers, whether it is a church setting or a home group, has a spiritual health or lack thereof. That condition exists based upon the individual hearts of those who gather together. Whatever the believers are filled with individually, the Church will be filled with collectively. An empty building contains no peace, joy, wisdom, or blessing, nor can there be unrest, bitterness, envy or strife present either. Church splits, in-fightings, contentions, debates, and lack of spiritual growth are eliminated when a group of believers, as a whole, are rightly related to the Lord. The Bible provides a sharp contrast represented by two local bodies of believers. The Corinthian church was in turmoil and confusion, perhaps on the verge of devastation, when Paul wrote to correct their situation. At the other extreme, the Church at Antioch was experiencing great prosperity in the Lord.

In comparing these two groups, we will learn much that can help enrich the local Body, provide healing where needed, bring unity, and make the Church a channel for the grace of God. He intends for his church to be a blessing Church, that is, increased and enriched by Him, and therefore able to do likewise to others.

Paul often wrote about the fullness that God intended for His people to possess. God's abundance includes being filled with the fullness of goodness (Rom. 15:14), the fulness of God (Eph. 3:19), the fulness of the fruits of righteousness (Phil. 1:11), and the fulness of the Spirit (Eph. 5:18). Too often the local Body is lacking in that which God intends; therefore, they are not able to do the work God would have them do. Since the Lord is always faithful to do His part, we must look to ourselves if a lack exists among us. Recognizing this lack is the first step to obtaining God's fullness. Confession of our need will bring God's supply.

Coming into right relationship with the Lord, giving Him the preeminence in our heart, constantly drawing our life and strength from Him, will infuse the Body with the life of God. Then the Body will prosper as the believers share the true communion of the Lord. None of us enters the Body of Christ as a mature, fruitful Christian able to minister to others. We come in with great need ourselves. As we are healed, strengthened, and edified in the Body setting, the Body as a whole is increased. Having been ministered to, we are then able to minister.

Unity of the Spirit is the God-ordained and blessed atmosphere for the Church. Unity of the Spirit provides for the life of God to flow from one member to another and then back again. Throughout this book, you will be given several illustrations of the blessing of the Lord that flowed from one member to another. These illustrations are but drops in the vast ocean of the love of God which is the source of the river of life that is to flow through us. Behold, how good and how pleasant it is for brethren to dwell together in unity! (Ps. 133:1)

It is not the intent of the author to deal with the outward structures of church government. Outward forms are corrected and infused with life when the members of the Body adhere to scriptural principles concerning their individual heart condition. My desire in writing this book is that you may be helped in becoming a supplying joint to the Body of Christ and that, through the Spirit's wonderful workings, you will be knitly joined together with believers of like precious faith.

No Other Foundation

I. The Draw Of God

The man who was sitting across from me that day in my office was under a powerful conviction of the Holy Spirit. He had been running from God for many years, but now he was being drawn unto Jesus by the Father. The softening in his heart was being reflected in the words he was speaking and the tears he was shedding. The drastic change in him was due to the revelation of the wretchedness of his own heart.

The tears of anguish were a welcome sight to the Heavenly Father who had wooed this man for such a long time. The work of God was laying a foundation in his heart. It is the foundation of repentance and brokenheartedness that all believers must have placed in them by the Spirit of God. This repentant man was at the door of great blessing: blessing that would flow into him and out through him to many others. How many lives would be touched by the Spirit of God that would now flow through this "new man"? How much of a supply would come through him to meet the needs of others? The dam of sin had been broken; a channel for the flow of the Spirit had been dug.

The goodness of God had led this man to repentance. The goodness of God would now flow into this vessel in ever increasing measure, limited only by his ability to receive of that goodness. He that spared not his own Son would now freely give to this one all that he needed. This man was now open to the Lord, and Jesus would become to him "wisdom, and righteousness, and sanctification, and redemption . . ."

If the local Body is to come into what God intends for it to possess, then the individuals of that local Body must have a correct foundation laid in them by God. Paul admonished the Corinthian church that only one foundation was chosen by God as the basis for His kingdom. That foundation is Jesus Christ. But how is that foundation properly laid in an individual's heart?

Our Lord stated quite plainly, "No man can come to me, except the Father which hath sent me draw him . . ." (John 6:44). Why is it necessary that the Father draw a man? The prophet Isaiah tells us:

"He (Jesus) hath no form nor comeliness; and when we shall see him, there is no beauty that we should desire him" (Isa. 53:2).

The Word does not say Jesus has no form or comeliness. It says He has none that we, blinded by carnality, would desire Him. We must learn that if God has chosen not to adorn the Lord in a form or comeliness that appeals to the carnal man, then neither should we. For if we appeal to the carnal man on the carnal level, we will bring carnality into the Church. How then can a man be saved? "No man can come to me, except the Father draw him!"

God's method of evangelism is His goodness expressed by His Church. That expression is seen in the believer's long-suffering, patience, kindness, mercy, faithfulness, and holiness. Paul tells us to overcome evil with good. That overcoming can be a lengthy process and quite costly. Saul of Tarsus was "overcome" by the goodness of God in the early Church. He saw it in Stephen and then in others he persecuted. The responses given to Saul by the Church became the pricks against which he kicked. The early Church had no gimmicks, no programs, no "celebrity testimonies," no "get-rich-quick" schemes. They did have the goodness of God filling their hearts. They had Jesus and He needs nothing added to Him.

Mother Teresa was speaking to persons who had come to meet her from all over the world. Among the groups to which she spoke was one of religious sisters from many North American orders. After her talk she asked if there were any questions. "Yes, I have one," a woman sitting near the front said. "As you know, most of the orders represented here have been losing members. It seems that more and more women are leaving all the time. Yet your order is attracting thousands upon thousands. What do you do?"

Without hesitating, Mother Teresa answered, "I give them Jesus."

"Yes I know," said the woman, "but take habits, for example. Do your women object to wearing habits? And the rules of the order, how do you do it?"

"I give them Jesus," Mother Teresa replied.

"Yes, I know, Mother," said the woman, "but can you be more specific?"

"I give them Jesus," Mother Teresa repeated again.

"Mother," said the woman, "We are all aware of your fine work. I want to know about something else."

Mother Teresa said quietly, "I give them Jesus. There is nothing else."

All the persecuted Church in China has to offer in evangelism is the goodness of God. And it is estimated that despite intense persecution, thousands of new believers are being added daily to its numbers. If we resort to an easy acceptance of Christ without repentance, then we do not have true conversions. We actually lead people away from the Lord rather than to Him. We are not to try to convert people to a doctrinal position, or try to convince them the Bible is true because of some recent archeological discoveries. We are to express the goodness of God. We are to lift up the Lord by expressing Him in our lives, and the goodness of God that men see will cause them to "glorify our Father in heaven."

God must draw a man out from where he lives on the carnal level of pride, self-sufficiency, self-justification, and rebellion. He will draw a man to where Jesus lives in humility and meekness and lowliness of mind. It is the "goodness of God that leadeth thee to repentance" (Rom. 2:4). That goodness is extended toward a man in many ways, but in particular, it is to be extended out from the Church. And to be so extended, it must first be contained in the Church. When one responds to the draw of God, he is brought to a place of repentance. Therein, he opens himself up to be filled, in ever increasing measure, with more of the goodness of God.

The goodness of God will lead a man to repentance by showing that man the sinfulness of his own heart. It is not a pleasant journey for such a man to come to Jesus Christ. He must be broken. He must be brought down. He must be devastated.

II. Blessed Devastation

If we are ever going to truly know God, we must be crushed by the revelation of the sinfulness of our own heart. This sinfulness of which I speak is our basic nature. It is a nature that cannot be subject to the law of God; it is a nature that is in rebellion to God.

Isaiah experienced this revelation and he cried, "Woe is me, . . . I am a man of unclean lips!" (Isa. 6:5). Jeremiah also discovered it in himself and said, "The heart (of man) is deceitful above all things, and desperately wicked . . ." (Jer. 17:9). The apostle Paul saw himself and cried out, "O wretched man that I am! who shall deliver me from the body of this death" (Rom. 7:24)? All who would be a part of the body "fitly joined together," must experience this devastation, for it is at this point that we begin to be "fitly joined" to the Body of Christ.

III. Repentance

While Paul was being brought to this place of devastation, he discovered that in his flesh dwelt no good thing. And it was not until he repented, that a "good thing" existed in him. Repentance is the firstfruit of all of the firstfruits of the Spirit. Repentance from dead works is the foundation of God's building in us. Repentance is the beginning of true righteousness. It is the first act of worshipping God in Spirit and in truth, preceding peace and joy in the Holy Ghost.

It is in this place of need that we, for the first time, see the beauty of the Lord Jesus Christ. It is in this place of needing a saviour, that our eyes are opened to see what they once could not see. Now we discover a "form and comeliness" that was in Jesus all the while. Here we begin to "see the King in his beauty" (Isa. 33:17). It is in this place of repentance that we begin to see the glory of God in the face of Jesus Christ.

> Repentance is the firstfruit of all of the firstfruits of the Spirit.

Repentance is the work of God upon which all other works of God are built. When we repent, we now have a good thing in us. That good thing is a broken heart and a contrite spirit. Such a heart contains a distrust of self, but great confidence in God. Now God has something in us upon which He can build, something in us He can shepherd, and something He can feed.

IV. Something To Build Upon

Our Lord does not commit Himself to us. He commits Himself to His work in us.

"Now when he was in Jerusalem at the passover, in the feast day, many believed in his name; when they saw the miracles which he did. But Jesus did not commit himself unto them, because he knew all men" (John 2:23-24).

Peter vowed he would not deny the Lord, but the Lord did not commit Himself to Peter. He knew Peter's vow came out of self-strength rather than from the work of God in him. Many make great commitments in times of emotional stirrings. But the kingdom of God is not built on emotional stirrings. It is built upon a work of God in the depths of a man's heart. It is a work that results in the breaking of the man's carnal strength and desires.

"For other foundation can no man lay than that which is laid, which is Jesus Christ" (1 Cor. 3:11). When a man repents, God has the foundation He has been seeking for in that man. Jesus told Peter, "When thou art converted, strengthen thy brethren" (Luke

22:32). The conversion would be one of Peter going from relying upon self-strength to having no confidence in the flesh. Such a man can "strengthen the brethren" because that man is founded upon the Rock, Christ Jesus. It is true this situation with Peter was not his initial conversion, but rather a "laying again the foundation of repentance from dead works" in Peter's heart (Heb. 6:1). Nevertheless, all spiritual progress is dependent upon having the correct foundation.

V. Something To Shepherd

"For ye were as sheep going astray; but are now returned unto the Shepherd and Bishop of your souls" (1 Pet. 2:25).

Self-will and self-justification have no room in a heart filled with humility and meekness. "The Lord is my shepherd" is then written upon the fleshly tables of our heart, and we begin to follow His leading. This returning requires a conversion from seeking our own will to submitting to God's will. Isaiah speaks concerning our straying:

"All we like sheep have gone astray; we have turned every one to his own way; and the LORD hath laid on him the iniquity of us all" (Isa. 53:6).

We strayed because of rebellion and wanting to fulfill our own desires. These things that caused us to go out of the way are dealt a death blow at our conversion. They are to have no place in our hearts or in the Church. Because we have returned to the Shepherd and Bishop of our soul, we are now partakers of all he can provide. More than that, we have an attitude, a heart condition, that enables us to be "shepherded." Without this brokenness, we would soon find ourselves once more far from the Shepherd. Many refuse to be broken and soon leave the sheepfold to seek pastures more to their liking.

VI. Something To Feed

Until we come to this place of brokenness and repentance, we do not have an appetite for the things of God. As surely as a natural born baby has an appetite for food, so too does a new-born babe in Christ have a hunger for the things of God. They have tasted and seen that the Lord is good. The need for the unleavened bread of sincerity and truth has been awakened. The hunger for the meat of the word will be developed in those who grow in God.

All of these characteristics of the new nature: having a foundation for God to build upon, following now the Shepherd, hungering for the things of God, find their origin in repentance.

What a wonderful foundation God has chosen upon which to build his Church. That foundation is always the basis of the building. It is never done away with. If we are going to build properly, we must build upon it—no other foundation ever— even for all eternity! That foundation of brokenheartedness must ever remain in the individuals in the local body of believers. As long as it exists in the hearts of the believers, the church will prosper in God.

VII. Abraham's Search

"For he looked for a city which hath foundations, whose builder and maker is God" (Heb. 11:10).

The Lord had said to Abraham, "Get thee out of thy country, and from thy kindred and from thy Father's house . . ." (Gen. 12:1). This Word of the Lord created in Abraham a separation from the things of this world. It was a separation that would continually grow. It also created a searching, a "looking for" in Abraham. He would watch to see if there was something or someone that would have the results of God's "get thee out" in them as well. He would look for those whose living had the same foundation as his. This foundation was the Word and work of God.

When Abraham returned from rescuing Lot, two kings met him. One was the king of Sodom. Abraham has nothing to do with him because the king of Sodom had nothing in him that could minister to the "get thee out" in Abraham. But the other King, Melchizedek, had much to offer him. In fact, the lesser (Abraham), was blessed by the greater (Melchizedek).

Not just anyone could bless Abraham. The "get thee out" in a believer must be ministered to on a certain level and by those who have the same "get thee out" of God in them. Abraham readily recognized the life of God in Melchizedek. He readily received what the "priest of the Most High God" put forth. The blessing of Melchizedek strengthened Abraham to reject the offer of the king of Sodom. Abraham recognized that Melchizedek had the same foundation for living that he had. The difference between the two men was that Melchizedek, at this point, had gone on further unto perfection than Abraham. It was a difference that Abraham inwardly acknowledged, because of the softness and humility of his heart.

This meeting of Melchizedek and Abraham was God-ordained and occurred at a certain time in Abraham's life. It happened after Abraham had "laid again the foundation of repentance" by building an altar to God. Abraham built this altar after his failure in Egypt (Gen. 12:9-20). He returned to the place where he "had made there an altar at the first" (Gen. 13:4).

Why did he build this altar? When God rescued him in Egypt, Abraham's eyes were opened to see the goodness and faithfulness of God to him personally. His heart was filled with thanksgiving and his faith renewed. He was able to see, if only dimly, the vision of what God could do in and for him. An altar is built because such elements as thanksgiving, faith, and vision fill a man's heart. A man of faith builds altars. In building these altars he confesses that he is a stranger and a pilgrim upon the earth. He sacrifices his natural life, with its affections, upon these altars. When we build altars, we say to the Lord, "You be the builder of my life."

VIII. Abraham's Sacrifice

Abraham offered up "spiritual sacrifices" to the Lord. He put upon the altar his sin and weakness that took him out of the will of God in the first place. He put his failures upon this altar. (Sometimes certain individuals find it very difficult to put their failures upon the altar. The cause for this difficulty may find its roots in self-righteousness and a secret desire to approach God on the basis of works.) When building this altar, Abraham added a renewed commitment to do the will of God for his life. He was saying, "To whatever extent I am able, I will pay the price necessary to do the will of God."

Now, with the foundation back in place in Abraham's life, it was time to go on unto perfection. God would permit Abraham's progress, and more than permit it, He would cause and aid it. Whatever Abraham would need, God would supply. That supply included the blessing of Melchizedek who brought forth bread and wine. The two would partake of the communion of the Lord.

God would have us once lay the foundation and be done with it. To do so saves the believer much time.

"Therefore, leaving the principles of the doctrine of Christ, let us go on unto perfection; not laying again the foundation of repentance from dead works, and of faith toward God. . . And this will we do, if God permit" (Heb. 6:1, 3).

With the foundation in place, we are now ready to move on in the purposes of God for our lives.

The man in my office that day was brought to a place of "blessed devastation." He confessed his sin because God had opened his eyes to see it. The dam of sin in this man's heart was broken up, and now out of "his innermost being" could flow rivers of living water. He spoke of the hunger he had for God's Word, of the need to be together with people of like precious faith. He was a changed man who was hearing the voice of God speak to him words of eternal life. The blessing was already evident. The foundation was laid. This man was filled with need for God. He was being fitly joined to the body of Christ.

Are Ye Not
Yet Carnal?

I. Paul's Difficult Task

In Paul's first epistle to the Corinthians, he told them, "And I brethren, could not speak unto you as unto spiritual, but as unto carnal, even as unto babes in Christ" (1 Cor. 3:1). There was in the Corinthian church all of the attitudes and sins you would find in a worldly situation. Ambition, envy, strife, division, vain glory, and confusion were all present through the people who made up that gathering of believers. Paul had to write a letter of correction, and he knew only those who were willing to repent would be able to receive his words. Since they were carnal, the likelihood was great that they would reject Paul's words.

Those who favored Apollos or Cephas over Paul could have rebelled and said, "Who does Paul think he is?" But Paul was going to supply that which was lacking in the Body and that which no one in Corinth seemed to be able to supply. Without this supply, the situation would not have been corrected. Matters in the church would have gone from bad to worse.

Paul, then, had the difficult task many ministers face, that is, trying to put a larger measure into a smaller one. Paul was spiritual, but he was speaking to those who were carnal. "The natural man receiveth not the receiveth not the things of the Spirit of God: for they are foolishness unto him" (1 Cor. 2:14).

Shortly after coming to the Lord, I attended a church in Pittsburgh, PA. The church was without a pastor at the time, so they asked a nearby Bible school to supply speakers for the services. One of the school's teachers who came to minister had just returned from missionary work in Peru for many years. His message lasted for about an hour, and when he was finished, I turned to my wife in frustration and said, "What in the world did that man say?" I had a college education and could normally understand most speakers, but this man left me mystified. But I will never forget watching him as he left the pulpit and walked to the back of the church. I knew in my spirit that he had something in God.

Shortly thereafter, during which time my wife and I answered the call of God to attend this same Bible school, I entered the classroom only to find this same minister as my teacher. And still, I did not understand him nor was I very open to receive what he had to say. My lack caused me to quit Bible school for about six months during which time I experienced great frustration. But after an intense breaking of my self-strength by the Lord, I returned to school. And again, I had this man as my teacher, but now I found myself able to receive what he had to say.

More than that, I could not get enough of what he had to say! Did he change in that time? No! It was I. My carnality, my self-strength was dealt a death blow by the Lord and I became open to receive from someone who had a much larger measure than myself. When one has been enlarged in his heart by the Lord (as this teacher had been), they are able to discern someone who has not yet had that same work done in them. They not only can discern that lack, but, because of their enlargement, they can patiently endure it as well.

Paul undertook the difficult task of putting his larger measure into the Corinthians' smaller measure. In writing his epistle, Paul knew the risks involved. If the Corinthians did not respond properly to his words of correction, he would be rejected and possibly asked never to come back. But it was a risk he was willing to take.

There is a difficulty involved in a spiritual man speaking to carnal people. Difficult, not for the spiritual man to put into words what he wants to say, but difficult for people of carnality to receive what is being said. It is easy to speak to spiritual people about spiritual things. Spiritual hearers aid the speaker in his bringing the message. Listeners who are hard-of-heart hinder the flow of the Spirit of God through the speaker. From week-to-week in the same church, the spiritual atmosphere and the ability of the people to hear can change. This ability to hear can even change from moment-to-moment in a given service!

In a situation that is charged with carnality, such as that which existed at Corinth, the only salvation is the preaching of the Word coupled with hearing hearts and repentance.

"Draw nigh to God, and he will draw nigh to you. Cleanse your hands, ye sinners; and purify your hearts, ye double-minded. Be afflicted and mourn, and weep: let your laughter be turned to mourning, and your joy to heaviness" (James 4:8-9).

Why would there be laughter and lightness in a gathering such as existed at Corinth? Because of self-strength prevailing through hardness of heart! The Word of the spiritual man, if received, would bring conviction resulting in sorrow of heart and tears. Then God would turn that sorrow into joy that would have a true godly basis. Paul's second letter to the Corinthians is cause for joy because they received his Word, sorrowed with godly sorrow, repented, and corrected the situation. Paul then commends them (See 2 Corinthians 7:11-16), and he is able to joy with them, because his difficult task had been accomplished.

II. Are Ye Not Yet Carnal?

"And I, brethren, could not speak unto you as unto spiritual, but as unto carnal, even as unto babes in Christ. I have fed you with milk, and not with meat: for hitherto ye were not able to bear it, neither yet now are ye able. For ye are yet carnal: for whereas there is among you envying, and strife, and divisions, are ye not carnal, and walk as men" (1 Cor. 3:1-3)?

Paul described himself as a wise masterbuilder and indeed he was. He knew what had to be done, and he knew the order in which it was to be done. That is why he spends the first two chapters of his letter contrasting the superiority of the wisdom of God to the wisdom of the world. He then says, "But we have the mind of Christ" (1 Cor. 2:16). He was referring to himself having the mind of Christ, in order that they would receive the wisdom he was about to give them. If the Corinthians had the mind of Christ, they were certainly not exercising it. As long as envy, strife, ambition, division, and debate are present in the Body, evidence exists that carnal thinking rules the members.

Paul found in the Corinthian church all the sins you would find in a worldly setting. In one instance, he tells them they had even "out-sinned" the heathens. The "world" filled this Church because worldly-thinking and worldly-affections filled the hearts and minds of its members. Envy, strife, ambition, and the like filled the church meetings because the members brought these things into the church.

What they brought into their gatherings caused them to leave with less spiritual strength than when they came. Many among them were sick and weak, and some were even spiritually dead. Paul would have been heartbroken over this situation because he knew God's intentions toward these and all believers:

"To whom God would make known what is the riches of the glory of this mystery among the gentiles; which is Christ in you, the hope of glory . . ." *(Col. 1:27).*

The riches of His glory! How rich is that? What a fullness God has promised to believers! But as long as we are carnal, we cannot contain the blessing and fullness of God. How does the Lord come and dwell in us (small vessels that we are) in all His fullness? He must conceal His glory from us because we cannot possibly take it in. He will continue to conceal His glory to us, until we are changed inwardly so as to be able to receive of His glory. It is while we abide in Him, that we come into a knowledge of God that is the result of the Lord revealing His glory to us.

John uses the phrase "we know" over and over in his first epistle. It is a knowledge obtained by abiding in and walking with the Lord. It is a knowledge of intimacy. Knowledge does not always love, but love will always have knowledge. It is a knowledge that comes by revelation of the treasures of the wisdom of God hidden in Jesus Christ.

When we obtain our knowledge in this way, we hold our knowledge correctly, because in order to obtain the revelation, our natural man must be mortified. The natural in us rejects the things of the Spirit of God. Such things are foolishness to an earthy man. But in following the Lord, that which is contrary in us to receiving from Him is consumed, allowing for a correct knowing. Such a knowledge does not result in our being puffed up, because it is only obtained in paths of humility and self-mortification. Religious books, Bible schools, theological seminaries, and even the Bible itself cannot in themselves impart such truths to our hearts. "Then said Jesus unto his disciples, If any man will come after me, let him deny himself, and take up his cross, and follow me" (Matt 16:24). A disciple is a student or a learner. The true knowledge of God to us personally occurs as we abide in Him and follow after Him.

> Knowledge does not always love, but love will always have knowledge.

III. The Mind Of Christ

We as individual believers are responsible for exercising the mind of Christ in our daily matters and in our relationships with one another.

"Let this mind be in you, which was also in Christ Jesus . . ." (Phil. 2:5).

Paul shows us that the Lord's thinking was always along the lines of humility and self-emptying.

"Who, being in very nature God, did not consider equality with God something to be grasped, but made himself nothing, taking the very nature of a servant, being made in human likeness" (Phil. 2:6-7, NIV).

Watch the Lord's descent! From being on an equality with God, the Lord descends to becoming a man, then a servant, then obedient to death, and not just any death, but the death of the cross. He who knew no sin was treated as if he were the sinner. This descending was His mindset. It is to be ours as well. This mindset is to characterize the Church.

Such a mindset does not exist in the world or in those who are conformed to this world. Before we came to the Lord we all thought like the world thinks. The world is always trying to become Number 1, to go to the highest heights. But we are to be transformed by the renewing of our mind (Rom. 12:1-3).

IV. A Vision

The following vision was related to me by its recepient, Thomas O'Brian while I was teaching a class at Pinecrest Bible Center. It illustrates the need for our thinking to be changed, as well as the ability of the Lord to change and enlarge us.

In 1985, after attending my present church for some three years, I received a startling vision from the Lord. In this vision, I found myself in the midst of other runners on a race track. Each of us had our own running lane and at the end of each lane was a crown. As I was running, I found myself being envious of the people in front of me and seemed to be hoping they would fall down so I could pass them. I looked to see those people behind me and found that I had a conceited attitude toward them. I then looked at the people on each side of me and felt more secure, but still somewhat provoked. Then the Lord told me, "You cannot run this race properly while you are looking at the other runners. I am going to put blinders on you." That he did! And the blinders were so restrictive, that I could only focus on the "race set before me" and the crown at the end of it.

When the vision ended I became very concerned with what the Lord was trying to tell me. I began to search the Scriptures, and through the Holy Spirit's leading, found myself reading Galatians 5:24-26, NIV: "Those who belong to Christ Jesus have crucified the sinful nature with its passions and desires. Since we live by the Spirit, let us keep in step with the Spirit. Let us not become conceited, provoking and envying each other." The Holy Spirit showed me that I had been judging the other members of our congregation as to their spiritual progress.

Over the next several months the Lord gave me many Scriptures that related to His position of judgment. All of these Scriptures helped me come to the following conclusion: judgment is not the prerogative of man, but discernment in the Holy Spirit is the responsibility of the believer.

Over the next several years, I tried desperately to work on my attitude toward others and to listen to the Holy Spirit so that I could "judge righteous judgment."

In 1988, I received the vision of the race once more. This time, as I was running, the blinders were gone, and I was praising God for the spiritual knowledge of the people in front of me. I was shouting words of encouragement to the people behind me, and I was smiling approvingly of the people on the sides of me. I thank God for his work in me, for before receiving the vision, my attitudes toward the brethren separated me from them. But since God has opened my eyes, He has knitly joined me together with people of like precious faith."

The truths in this vision may reflect attitudes we ourselves have harbored before God did His work in us as well. They certainly reflect the disciples' hearts while the Lord was with them before His crucifixion.

V. Are Ye Yet Without Understanding

"And they (The disciples) understood none of these things: and this saying was hid from them, neither knew they the things which were spoken" (Luke 18:34).

How could the disciples have understood the mind of the Lord when they were going one direction (up), and He was going the other direction (down)? In Mark 9:33 the Lord asked the disciples a question concerning certain discussions they had and were having (even during the Last Supper). The discussions centered around who was going to have the highest position, the most honor, the most power when the Lord established His kingdom.

Because of those attitudes, the disciples created divisions among themselves and caused their hearts to be hardened. Because they did not have a mindset like the Lord's, they could not understand His words. Jesus knew how they thought; therefore, there were many things He did not even try to tell them (John 16:12).

But there came a time when they could understand:
"When therefore he was risen from the dead, his disciples remembered that he had said this unto them; and they believed the Scripture, and the word which Jesus had said" (John 2:22).

Their understanding, however, was not based upon a time element; but rather, a drastic change in their heart condition brought about by their suffering through the "losing" of their Messiah to the crucifixion.

VI. The Wisdom Of God Or Man?

"For I determined not to know any thing among you, save Jesus Christ, and him crucified" (1 Cor. 2:2).

This determination of Paul governed his words, actions, attitudes, and motivations. Paul had made this determination because of the work of the grace of God in him. Paul became very narrow-minded in the very best sense. He wanted the Corinthians to be of the same mind as he. He wanted his determination to be their determination, especially in relating to one another. James speaks about friendship with the world being enmity with God. If we apply the wisdom of the world to our actions and attitudes concerning one another, we will not be working with God but against Him.

It is essential for those who desire to work with God to have the wisdom of this world reduced to nothing in their hearts. That is why Paul asks the question, "Where is the wise? where is the scribe, where is the disputer of this world" (1 Cor. 1:20)? His answer was, "They are not in my heart, they have been displaced by a revelation of the value of the wisdom of God." Discovering the wisdom of God that is hidden in Jesus Christ brings us to the place of seeing the foolishness of the wisdom of this world. When God says, "I will destroy the wisdom of the wise, and bring to nothing the understanding of the prudent," (1 Cor. 1:19), He is telling us of the work He will do in the hearts of His people. He will destroy the wisdom of the wise on the universal level, to be sure. But the first place that work is to be done is in our hearts, so that the wisdom of the world has no place in the Church.

Where is the disputer of this world? He is in the political arena, the educational arena, in the sports arena. He has been given an exalted position in the hearts of men. He has crept into Christian gatherings. Even Paul found him there, for he warns Timothy:

"But shun profane and vain babblings: for they will increase unto more ungodliness" (2 Tim. 2:16).

What room does this admonition of Paul leave for political debate, sports discussions, or worldly talk shows? If we engage in these things, we operate and increase in self-strength. What then should we be occupied with? Paul supplies the answer:

"Till I come, give attendance to reading, to exhortation, to doctrine. Meditate upon these things; give thyself wholly to them; that thy profiting may appear to all" (1 Tim. 4:13,15).

Paul equates giving ourselves to the correct things with spiritual profiting. Such people are then able to increase the Church with the blessings they have received by heeding Paul's words. Much profit is lost to the Church because members spend so much time in unprofitable activities.

How will we deal with our enemies, our difficulties, and trials? According to the wisdom of the world or according to the wisdom of God? Enemies and trials will take us further into God if we respond to them in the wisdom of God. When we act according to the wisdom of God toward our enemies, we war after the Spirit and not the flesh.

The strength of man in the form of Roman soldiers, Jewish religious leaders, and devil-inspired attackers warred against the weakness of God in Jesus Christ. They used every weapon available to them to bring him down out of the love and grace of God and have him respond in carnal ways. But they could not bring him down to their level where they could have defeated him. He remained in the weakness of God and defeated the strength of men at Calvary.

For the first part of the twentieth century, even until the 1970's, many Pentecostal Bible schools resisted the mixing of the wisdom of the world and the wisdom of God. The result of this resistance was the development of able ministers of the gospel who, out from these schools, "went and preached Christ."

But slowly, one by one, these same schools have succumbed to the temptation to "be like the other nations (schools) around them." And now the ministers being produced from these schools know little, if anything, of "Jesus Christ and Him crucified." And the Church suffers from this deviation from God's ways.

What we then have (when man's knowledge is given the preeminence) is the knowledge of God held within the context of the knowledge of man. Therefore, the knowledge of God is out of its correct context. The knowledge of God must encompass and swallow up all other knowledge. Such a knowledge can only be produced in us by the work of God. "I will destroy the wisdom of the wise!" When that work is done in our hearts, we will not seek what the wise of this world seek, we will not value what they value. We will discard the methods the world employs. The mind of Christ will lead us to walk contrary to those who are trained in this world's thinking, and the mind of Christ will have the preeminence in the Church.

When the wisdom of this world has been destroyed in our hearts and we have received the Spirit of God, we will be able to see and know the "things that are freely given to us of God." We will be able to receive what the world cannot, for we will highly value what the world considers foolishness:

"But the natural man receiveth not the things of the Spirit of God: for they are foolishness unto him: neither can he know them, because they are spiritually discerned. But he that is spiritual judgeth all things, yet he himself is judged of no man" (1 Cor. 2:14-15).

The "treasures of the wisdom of the knowledge of God hid in Jesus Christ" will then be held in our hearts. The riches of God will then be ready to be communicated to one another to enrich the Church.

VII. Why Do You Not Allow Yourselves To Be Defrauded?

Without the mind of Christ being allowed to operate in the Body, we will never come into that which God intends for us to have. As long as carnal thinking dominates the Church, we will find the same sins in the church that exist in worldly situations.

"Dare any of you, having a matter against another, go to law before the unjust, and not before the saints" (1 Cor. 6:1)?

Paul dealt with this fault in Corinth on two levels. The first level is good, but the second is a "more excellent way." 1 Corinthians 6:1-6 instructs us to seek out wise men who are able to give godly judgment and declare who is right in a given matter. That is a better course of action than what many people do in the Church when they are offended by a brother or sister. Often times, brethren of today will do what the Corinthians were doing: that is, taking their brethren to court, even before unbelievers.

How does one do that today? By speaking against a brother or sister to someone who is of the world! And why is such a thing done? — for self justification! The offended brother wants to be judged innocent in a matter and wants the offending brother to be judged guilty. Such actions do not find the mind of Christ as their source.

"Speak not evil one of another, brethren. He that speaketh evil of his brother, and judgeth his brother, speaketh evil of the law, and judgeth the law: but if thou judge the law, thou art not a doer of the law, but a judge" *(James 4:11).*

James was dealing with the same problem in his group as Paul faced with the Corinthians. This problem was not uncommon then, nor is it now. But we are called to be doers of the law and not judges of it. As soon as we judge and condemn another brother, we make ourselves usurpers. We take to ourselves a position that belongs to God alone. There is one Judge and one Lawgiver. It is our place to fulfill the righteousness of the law, not judge (and condemn) others.

"I can of mine own self do nothing: as I hear, I judge: and my judgment is just; because I seek not mine own will, but the will of the Father which hath sent me" (John 5:30).

If we receive the judgment of God concerning another, we must only apply it under the direction of the Spirit of God and in love. We are not to judge another in order to save ourselves suffering, or to judge unto condemnation.

Condemnation of others will not meet whatever lack may truly exist in their hearts. God did not send His Son to condemn the world, but rather to save it. The Lord told His disciples "As my Father hath sent me, even so send I you" (John 20:21). Therefore, if we are involved in judgment and condemnation we are not workers together with the Lord in his work. (See 2 Corinthians 6:1-3)

After Elijah called fire down from heaven, he expected to be heartily received by the people. When threatened by Jezebel, he became overwhelmed with disappointment. He then began to pray. This prayer of Elijah was unlike his prayer concerning rain (See James 5:17). Although Elijah was a man subject to like passions as we are, his prayer concerning rain did not come out of his passions, but rather from the will of God. However, his prayer concerning the people of Israel at this time, does originate from his passions and from his desire for justification. Paul says in Romans 11:2-4 that Elijah made intercession **against** Israel.

"And he said, I have been very jealous for the LORD God of hosts: for the children of Israel have forsaken thy covenant, thrown down thine altars, and slain thy prophets with the sword; and I, even I only, am left; and they seek my life, to take it away" (1 Kings 19:10).

Elijah was indeed a man subject to like passions as we. And some of his prayers were said while he was in subjection to those passions and some were not. We never pray correctly when we pray out of subjection to our carnal passions.

Notice his prayer begins with "I." He then enters evidence into court against God's people. His evidence is to a great extent, true. But God does not want him taking the people to a court of law — even God's law. God wants these people to be brought before the throne of grace. Elijah made intercession against Israel; Moses made intercession for Israel. Elijah was unknowingly condemning "7,000" faithful people. When we speak evil of a brother or sister, we are making intercession against them (and against ourselves as well).

James gets to the heart of the matter:
"But if ye have bitter envying and strife in your hearts, glory not, and lie not against the truth. This wisdom descendeth not from above, but is earthly, sensual, devilish" (James 3:14-15).

If the wisdom we exercise in the Church and in our personal relationships is not from the mind of Christ, how are we going to accomplish God's purposes for and through us? James is saying, "Do not praise, sing, or make vows of love to God if envy, bitterness, and strife fill your heart. "Glory not! And lie not against the truth." What truth? The truth to which the Spirit of God is witnessing concerning our heart condition.

It is true that God inhabits the praises of His people, but only when those praises come out of correct and pure hearts. Paul tells the Corinthians:

"Your glorying is not good. Know ye not that a little leaven leaveneth the whole lump?" (1 Cor. 5:6)

"And ye are puffed up, and have not rather mourned, that he that hath done this deed might be taken away from among you" (1 Cor. 5:2).

Paul is telling the Corinthians that any outward religious activity is all in vain if the foundation is not correct. More than that, the communion of the Body is tainted by the leaven of sin, which results in the Body being weakened. When the wisdom of the world is operating in the Church, "There is confusion and every evil work" (James 3:16). There are also misdirected prayers, as well as laughter and rejoicing out of self-strength and hearts lifted up in pride. So then, in order to correct the situation, the condition must be exposed. And those who are guilty of it must repent so that the Spirit of God can flow once again in their midst.

VIII. The More Excellent Way

Paul had given one solution to the disputes that arise in the Church. They can be resolved by the judgments of wise men. But there is a higher level of action:

"Now therefore there is utterly a fault among you, because ye go to law one with another. Why do ye not rather take wrong? Why do ye not rather suffer yourselves to be defrauded?" (1 Cor. 6:7)

It is most interesting that the word "fault" means "diminishing" or "deterioration." Remember that the Church came together, not for the better, but for the worse. This deterioration could be seen in the level of communion among them. There would be spiritual regression rather than progression.

Paul asked the question, "Why do you not rather take wrong?" Paul knew the answer to his question; he was trying to make the Corinthians see the cause of their lack. It was caused by their not exercising the mind of Christ. And when we do not exercise the mind of Christ in such matters, we will seek self-justification and vindication. We will be unwilling to pay the price in any given matter. But someone in the Church must be willing to pay the price. The Lord paid the price; He desires we would follow His example.

The Church can only be enriched when we empty ourselves of self. The Lord was the only one who deserved fair treatment, but he chose to lay aside his rights. When we receive Christ as saviour we are to yield our rights to Him. We are not our own, we are bought with a price. Our rights are now His rights. He can choose to use them as He wills. As long as we insist upon our rights, our eyes will be blinded to the glory of God. How far do you suppose Joseph would have progressed had he held onto his rights? Rights, incidentally, that would have been justified in a court of law! Our being able to bless the Church is based upon our spiritual progress, and our spiritual progress is directly related to our laying aside our rights. We see numerous examples of Paul being defrauded by the "brethren," but it did not deter him from laying down his life to meet their need.

It was Paul who exhorted the Thessalonians to "rejoice evermore" and "in everything give thanks." The meaning of "rejoice evermore" is literally, "rejoice every **when**." When you are lied about, rejoice. When you are mistreated, rejoice. When you are defrauded, or misjudged, or rejected, **rejoice**! Rejoice every "when," and in everything give thanks. For the Lord, Himself, gave thanks even in the night He was betrayed. There is great power released in our lives when we carry such attitudes. We must have a surrender to and a confidence in the ability of God to work everything for our good. If we have such a confidence, then we will rejoice every "when"; we will in everything give thanks; we will experience victory after victory, and we will minister life to all the situations we encounter.

Did the Corinthians pray subject to their passions or subject to the will of God? James corrected his group's praying with these words:

"Ye ask, and receive not, because ye ask amiss, that ye may consume it upon your lusts" (James 4:3).

James says, "Ye have not!" That is, you do not have that which can bless others. If worldly thinking rules us, we must go before the Lord and confess our sin. When we do that, our prayers change from being self-centered to being filled with concern for others. When we exercise the mind of Christ, our asking is corrected. When our asking is corrected, we are able to receive. Having received, we are able to bless. James tells us we are to be doers of the Word, not judges. Let us not forsake our responsibility in this matter, for the Lord's coming was that the righteousness of the law might be fulfilled in those who walk after the Spirit.

3

The Judgment Seat of Christ: NOW!

I. Submitting To Judgment

The importance of allowing ourselves to be judged by the Lord is impossible to overstate. The benefits derived from that judgment comprise the kingdom of God in our hearts. The Lord is the door and all those who would enter into the kingdom of God must pass through Him. All spiritual progress is based upon receiving the judgments of the Lord in the various forms that they take: Correction, edification, exhortation, rebuke and the like.

"For the time is come that judgment must begin at the house of God: and if it first begin at us, what shall the end be of them that obey not the gospel of God?" (I Peter 4:17)

We are told in the book of Hebrews not to harden our hearts when we hear the Lord's voice as the Israelites did in their wandering in the wilderness. What is the nature of the Lord's voice? It is a voice of salvation, edification, correction, comfort, enabling, mercy, long suffering, and life.

David declared that the testimonies of the Lord, His judgments, His Law (or flow) are, "more to be desired than gold, yea than much fine gold." David realized the value of the judgments and testimonies of the Lord because his advance into the kingdom of God was due to his submitting to them.

The following illustration gives us the changes that take place in us at the judgment seat of Christ. (When I speak of this judgment seat, I am not referring to the final judgment, but rather, to the present judgments of the Lord in our lives that will cause the final judgment to be a place of reward and joy for all those who hear His voice daily).

THE LORD'S JUDGMENT

From:	Unto:
Corruption	Incorruption
Blindness	Vision and discernment
Spiritual ignorance	Knowledge of God
Death	Life
Self centered misjudgments	Righteous judgment without partiality
Demand for justice	Full of mercy
Worldliness & earthiness	Sanctification
False witness	Faithful and true witness

Before we receive the Lord into our heart, we are filled with those things mentioned in the left hand column. It is at the judgment seat of Christ that we pass out of those things and into the list on the right. We can see this truth very readily in the gospels.

We are told in the gospel of Luke that the Samaritans rejected the Lord, "Because His face was as though He would go to Jerusalem." His disciples James and John were very upset over this treatment:

"And when his disciples James and John saw this, they said, Lord, wilt thou that we command fire to come down from heaven, and consume them, even as Elias did?" (Luke 9:54)

James and John presented themselves "at the judgment seat of Christ" to obtain the approval to rid themselves of these "enemies." What was their inward condition when they approached the Lord? They came in spiritual blindness and ignorance, and with a spirit contrary to and unlike the Lord's. When Jesus came He condemned or judged sin in the flesh. Since He is the same yesterday, today, and forever, He is still condemning sin in the flesh. That is, He will judge it in our flesh. And when we agree with His judgment and confess our sin, He will cleanse us from our unrighteousness. The Lord's response to James and John was this: Luke 9:55-56, "But he turned, and rebuked them, and said, Ye know not what manner of spirit ye are of. For the Son of man is not come to destroy men's lives, but to save them. And they went to another village."

Neither James nor John learned this truth in a previous teaching by the Lord. They were there when the Lord gave the sermon on the mount. His teaching included, "But I say unto you, Love your enemies, bless them that curse you, do good to them that hate you, and pray for them which despitefully use you, and persecute you," Matthew 5:44. We are like these disciples, in that what we do not learn in the classroom may have to be learned in the circumstances of life. The Lord is a good teacher who will repeat the same lesson in another way. The softer our hearts, the less severe the lesson needs to be.

A key word in the above verses is "destroy." The Lord uses it in relationship to men's lives and applies it to those who were at that time opposing Him. Despite their rejection of Him, He remains faithful to them, always looking to bring salvation and life to those in need. But there is one who does intend to destroy men's lives, and that one is Satan.

II. The Marred Image

Satan had a 3-fold purpose in mind when he approached Adam and Eve in the Garden.

He intended to:

1. STEAL God's creation, man.
2. KILL the relationship of man to God
3. DESTROY the image of God witnessed to by God's creation, man.

45

Knitly Joined Together

Paul, in Romans 1:29-31 describes the extent of the enemy's work in the hearts of men.

"Being filled with all unrighteousness, fornication, wickedness, covetousness, maliciousness; full of envy, murder, debate, deceit, malignity; whisperers, Backbiters, haters of God, despiteful, proud, boasters, inventors of evil things, disobedient to parents, Without understanding, covenant breakers, without natural affection, implacable, unmerciful:" (Rom 1:29-31)

These characteristics are so contrary to the image of God. Paul tells us earlier in Romans that man changed the glory of God (That is, the glory of God that was inherent in His original creation of man) and made it like "corruptible man, and to birds, and to fourfooted beasts, and creeping things." That is why Jesus addressed Herod as a fox. And that is why John the Baptist called the scribes and pharisees, "vipers." And in Psalm 22, we see that strong bulls and dogs are accosting the psalmist and, prophetically, the Lord during His crucifixion. Thus, the image of God has been destroyed in man by the cooperation of man with Satan.

But Jesus is come to seek and to save that which was lost. He does so by winning back the heart of man that has been stolen by Satan and has been made a servant of sin. He leads the saved one on paths of righteousness and restoration. As the relationship with God grows and deepens, the man is changed back from "a lie into the truth." The man is then conformed to the image of God and becomes a true and faithful witness to God.

When we are change into the image of God, we too will seek to save men's lives, not destroy them. This transformation takes place as we submit ourselves to the judgments of the Lord.

Paul tells us in Corinthians that as we have borne the image of the earthy, so too will we bear the image of the heavenly. How did we come to the place of bearing the image of the earthy? We were birthed into life with that earthly nature. Then that nature was ministered to and we grew and developed and matured. In like manner, will we bear the heavenly image. We must be born again or birthed from above, or must be given the life from above. As that life is ministered to in us , we grow and develop, and mature.

As we submitted ourselves to numberless judgments concerning the earthly nature, so too must we submit ourselves to the judgments of the Lord concerning the new nature. These judgments are clothed in the mercy of God.

"Justice and judgment are the habitation of thy throne: mercy and truth shall go before thy face" (Psalm 89:14).

God dwells in a light unto which no man can approach. This light is comprised of His judgments and justice. None of us, in our own strength and righteousness, can possibly approach this habitation of God. We must be dealt with in mercy and then changed by that mercy. It is only when we are immersed in His mercy that we are able to receive His truth which then changes the marred image into His image. Before Adam sinned, he testified to God simply by being what God had created him. He was a true witness. He looked like his creator. But when he sinned, he no longer reflected the image of the creator. He became a false witness. And all men who are filled with the sin described by Paul in Romans 1:29-31 stated above, are also found to be false witnesses.

But Jesus comes to restore the lost image of God in man and to change the lie, the false witness, back into the truth. And we cooperate with Him by agreeing with His judgments. It is the nature of the carnal man to judge (or better put, misjudge) everything. But Paul warns us,

"Therefore judge nothing before the time, until the Lord come, who both will bring to light the hidden things of darkness, and will make manifest the counsels of the hearts: and then shall every man have praise of God" (1 Cor. 4:5).

What Paul is telling us to do is always wait until the Lord reveals His judgment on a given matter and then agree with it. So then, in reality, we never judge; we only agree with the Lord's judgment.

"Let God be true, but every man a liar; as it is written, That thou mightest be justified in thy sayings, and mightest overcome when thou art judged" (Romans 3:4).

We have seen that the habitation of the throne of God is justice and judgment. No man has ever come near to that glory on his own merits except the Lord Jesus. By his sinless life, He has entered in to the full glory and presence of the Most High God. In so doing, He was/is filled with all the treasures of the wisdom and knowledge of God. He contains the perfect combination of justice and judgment, therefore all judgment is committed unto the Son.

We are instructed to "come boldly to the **throne of grace**." But Jesus is "set on the right hand of the **throne of the Majesty in the heavens**." These two thrones constitute two very different places in the spirit. We can go to the one, that is, the throne of grace. But the throne of the Majesty in the heavens is inaccessible to us apart from us being led there by the one mediator between man and God, the man Christ Jesus. And our spiritual progress along that way is totally dependent upon our receiving the judgments of the Lord to us personally. "Let us go on to perfection! And this we will do if God permit!" Why would He not permit it? Because we have not yielded to certain judgments.

The justice and judgment that is the habitation of the throne of God comprise the everlasting burnings spoken of in Isaiah 33:14 and are referred to by the writer of Hebrews when he speaks of our God "being a consuming fire." No flesh shall glory in His presence because it will be consumed as a man enters deeper and deeper into the center of that presence.

III. But I Say Unto You

Because of the Lord's yielding to all of His Father's judgments without fail, He has obtained and knows all the judgments of God. His words are spirit and life; made so, by His obedience to God. He taught with the authority that comes from personal experience:

"Ye have heard that it hath been said, An eye for an eye, and a tooth for a tooth: BUT I SAY UNTO YOU, That ye resist not evil: but whosoever shall smite thee on thy right cheek, turn to him the other also" (Matthew 5:38-39).

"An eye for an eye!" Where did man get that? Have you ever heard someone in the world say that? It is justice and judgment. An eye for an eye! But the Lord did not relate to God or man after the law, but rather by mercy and truth. He was not a son by religion but by relationship. And out from this relationship, He learned the heart of His Father. He declares the heart of God to us.

He, himself, was sent from the heart of God:

"For God so loved the world, that He gave His only begotten Son, that whosoever believeth in Him should not perish, but have everlasting life" (John 3:16)

Too often, we glibly quote this verse without considering the implications. God gave His blessed, Holy, Harmless Son to a vicious world, to sinners of great degradation; and they abused Him and killed Him. He paid a price beyond our ability to comprehend it. And that price was paid daily during His life here on earth. "He learned obedience by the things He suffered. And being made perfect . . ." He was not born perfect. That is, He was not the express image of His Father until the cross. But every day, while here on earth, He moved closer and closer to being the express image of the Father. That is why He had to drink the cup. He had prayed, "if it be possible, let this cup pass from me." This prayer was made with strong crying and with tears and He was heard by the Father. (See Hebrews 5:7) And although the answer of the Father is not recorded in Scripture, there are certain implications of what may have been said:

"Son, if you want to be delivered, the angels are at your disposal. If you decide to call for them they will deliver you. You look so much like me now, far more than any other man has ever looked. But if you want to look just like me, if you want to be my express image, so that when I look at you it is as though I am looking in the mirror, you must drink the cup. If you want to reveal all of my heart to mankind, and if you want to enter into my full presence where no other being has ever been before, you must drink the cup."

Hebrews 5:8-9 adds:
"Though he were a Son yet learned he obedience by the things which he suffered; And being made perfect, he became the author of eternal salvation unto all them that obey him;"

He was not perfected until He suffered and died on the cross. It was the culmination of His spiritual progress which brought Him to the end of the path of the just and to the light of the "perfect day."

And out from that spiritual progress and from that relationship with His Father came His, "But I say unto you." Those words were His judgments. And they were filled with mercy and truth. Why?

"Justice and judgment are the habitation of thy throne: mercy and truth shall go before thy face" (Psalm 89:14).

He was filled with justice and judgment but, because he knew the heart of His Father, He approached people with mercy and truth. It is this mercy that enables us to make spiritual progress in the way the Lord Himself walked.

IV. Go And Learn

"The earth, O LORD, is full of thy mercy: teach me thy statutes" (Psalms 119:64).

How much of the earth is filled with our mercy? Could we fill the city in which we live with mercy? The church we attend? Our homes? Another's heart? We delight in receiving mercy, but we are not very ready in the natuaral to give mercy. Yet the Lord remonstrated with the pharises:

"But go ye and learn what that meaneth, I will have mercy, and not sacrifice: for I am not come to call the righteous, but sinners to repentance" (Matthew 9:13).

Where must we go to learn the truth Jeremiah declared concerning the Lord, that He is a God "that exercises loving kindness, judgment, and righteousness in the earth, for in these things I delight, saith the Lord." The Lord's delight is to extend mercy to those in need. Therefore, we rob the Lord of that delight when we fail to recognize our sin that He judges. We learn this truth that God would have mercy instead of sacrifice as we allow the Lord to search our hearts and expose the corruption in them and the need for His mercy.

When we truly see that need, we are brought to confession and to a place of justifying God in His sayings (concerning us). See Romans 3:4. Our mouth is then stopped in relationship to condemning others for we see our own sin and the need for mercy. Having been judged, and having received mercy, we are then able to give that mercy to others.

When the judgments of the Lord come to us, we are crushed by the weight of His words. Our knee then bows to Him and we "become guilty before God." This word "guilty" can be rendered: "Subject to the judgment of God." Being in subjection to the judgment of God is the entrance way into great blessing. It is here that we receive the mercy of God and His justification into our heart. This justification is the only thing that will satisfy our need for mercy. The pharisee justified himself before God by his good works. But God did not justify him because by the works of the law shall no flesh be justified. The publican, however, called upon the name of the Lord to forgive him because he was a sinner. His confession was heard, and the Lord declared concerning him, "I tell you this man went down to his house justified rather than the other . . ." Luke 18:14

The divine order then is judgment, mercy, and faith:

"Woe unto you scribes and Pharisees, hypocrites! For ye pay tithe of mint and anise and cummin, and have omitted the weightier matters of the law, judgment, mercy, and faith: these ought ye to have done, and not to leave the other undone" (Matthew 23:23).

Faith is a result of our receiving mercy because we then come into fellowship and right relationship with the Lord. It is easy to believe after we have received mercy because the Lord authors our faith in that place. One day I received a call from a woman who had been gloriously delivered by the Lord. As she spoke, it was easy to hear that she did so from a heart filled with mercy and the faith that works by love. She had been involved in immorality. But the Lord visited her and spoke one word to her. She said, "When the Lord spoke that word to me, it hit me like a ton of bricks." That is very scriptural because the words of the Lord carry great power and authority. And judgment is one of the weightier matters of the law.

Not only do those words convict, they convert because they are part of the flow of the river of life that constantly comes from God, Himself.

"The law of the LORD is perfect, converting the soul: the testimony of the LORD is sure, making wise the simple" (Psalms 19:7).

The word for law could be interpreted "flow." That which is flowing out of the Lord is perfect. It is complete, it is entire, it is lacking nothing. It is that flow that causes the earth to be filled with the mercy of the Lord. And it is that flow that converts and restores souls. And when we submit to the judgment of God and receive His mercy, we begin to flow with Him.

Jonah was a prophet of God. Yet he never truly entered into that flow of the Lord. He had the message of God concerning the Ninevites, but he did not have the heart of God. If we have the heart of God we will carry the message of God. After being swallowed by the fish, and because he was in rebellion to God, it took Jonah three days and three nights before he prayed to the Lord for deliverance. When the Lord extended mercy to Jonah, he was very glad. Glad to receive God's mercy, but not glad to give it to the Ninevites. He was filled with sef justification even to the point of accusing God.

"And he prayed unto the LORD, and said, I pray thee, O LORD, was not this my saying, when I was yet in my country? Therefore I fled before unto Tarshsish: for I knew that thou art a gracious God, and merciful, slow to anger, and of great kindness, and repentest thee of the evil" (Jonah 4:2).

He knew the heart of God, but he was not willing to enter into that flow. And it seems that he never did, because the book of Jonah ends very abruptly. Why? Because all of the paths of the Lord are mercy and truth, and Jonah was not in agreement with God. And how can two walk together except they be agreed?

Isaiah, on the other hand, received the judgment of God concerning himself and he declared:

"Then said I, Woe is me! For I am undone; because I am a man of unclean lips, and I dwell in the midst of a people of unclean lips: for mine eyes have seen the King, the LORD of hosts" (Isaiah 6:5).

In this place of judgment and confession, God extends mercy to the prophet. Then a call is given as to ministry concerning this same people of unclean lips. Knowing what these people are like, why would Isaiah answer the call? Because he had received mercy in regard to the very same condition as to the people to whom he was called to minister. It was a ministry that would require great mercy because they were going to reject the message and the messenger until the very message that should have softened their hearts made their hearts hard. See Isaiah 6:8-11.

It was Jonah who declared:
"They that observe lying vanities forsake their own mercy" (Jonah 2:8).

Yet he was guilty of that very thing. We must be very careful not to deceive ourselves. David could declare, "Surely goodness and mercy shall follow me all the days of my life," because he was following the good shepherd. And as he received the mercy of the Lord, he would give it out as well. Therefore, he left behind him goodness and mercy. We are to do the same, and it is at the judgment seat of Christ that we receive mercy and therefore are able to have it follow us all the days of our lives.

V. The Benefits Of The Judgments Of The Lord

We can only give an overview of some of the many benefits of the judgment seat of Christ. Before we pass through His judgments we are of the earth, earthly. We are filled with corruption. But when we receive His judgments, we are transformed from the earthly to the heavenly. This corruptible then puts on incorruption. And lest you think we must wait until we physically die for that to occur, let us again consider the situation with James and John wanting to call fire down from heaven.

You will remember they came in spiritual ignorance and with an "unChristlike" spirit. The judgment of the Lord was quite a rebuke to them. It must have gone into John like a knife. But it was such an effective two edged sword, for it not only killed the earthly in John, it caused him to see the Lord and thus come into life. And as we read his first epistle we see over and over the phrase, "We know." He no longer is living in spiritual ignorance. And more than that, he states, "We know that we have passed from death unto life . . ." He was speaking about his corruptible putting on incorruption. The revelation stated in John 3:16 itself probably came out of this incident with the Samaritans and the Lord's rebuke to him.

Until we pass through the judgment seat of Christ it is impossible for us to fulfill the Lord's command to "judge righteous judgment." We are too self-centered to do that. We are too much filled with self love. We are easily offended, and we demand justice. (That is, we are quick to demand justice FOR ourselves, but not so quick to give justice OUT FROM ourselves.)

We operate in the wisdom that is from beneath. Since we are of the earth, earthly, we resort to the wisdom that is earthly, sensual, and even devilish. It is not until we allow the Lord to judge these things in us that we can operate in the wisdom that is from above. (See James 3:15-17)

The wisdom that is from above is first "pure." We must be purified from the corruption of sin in our lives. When that takes place, we have peace with God and we can trust Him to care for us and protect us without our having to do so. If someone defrauds us, we do not demand justice. We do not "go to war" to get justice. We rest in God. We believe He will work all things together for our good. If one lies about us, we suffer it because we are at peace. And we do not let the sinful actions of others disturb that peace.

We, in contrast to those Paul describes in Romans 1:29-31 as being "implacable," are "easy to be intreated." One who is implacable will not give an inch. They will demand justice. They will win every argument (even if they don't really win them). But the one who is easy to be intreated does not argue. They readily yield the right of way to others. They give up their ground as did Abraham when dealing with Lot. Remember his words? "Let there be no strife, I pray thee, between me and thee . . . for we be brethren." Why did he say such a thing? After all, he was more in the right than Lot.

Abraham had received the judgments of God to him personally. He operated in the wisdom from above and he became easy to be intreated. Have you ever considered, in light of the earth being the

Lord's and the fulness thereof, how much ground God has yielded? Why? He is easy to be intreated.

And what is in the head should certainly be in the body. So that we, as members of the body of Christ, should operate in the wisdom that is from above. Not only is this wisdom pure, peaceable, and easy to be intreated, it is also full of mercy. At the judgment seat of Christ we become guilty before God and need mercy. It is at the judgment seat of Christ that we obtain mercy. Paul speaks of being one "who obtained mercy." And his life and words constantly reflected one who was "full of mercy."

The next benefit mentioned by James concerning the wisdom that is from above is so unlike the earthly wisdom most use. James tells us that God's wisdom is without partiality. We are so partial to so many things. But if we discover the roots of our partiality, we will see they are firmly planted in the soil of self love.

"My family, my children, my church, my pastor, my union, my denomination, my country, my, O my, O my!" Many speak of desiring the unity of the early church. How did they obtain such unity? They passed through the judgment seat of Christ where he condemned their sin in their flesh. They had to confess their strife and partiality and schisms. And in so doing, they came to the place where there was one Lord, one faith, etc. They had to forsake the desire to be the greatest in the kingdom. That motivation was consumed by the fire of the Lord's judgment. They were purified from that and much more and they entered into peace with one another. Such oneness occurs only by our passing through the judgment seat of Christ.

Yet another quality spoken of by James concerning the wisdom from above is that it is "without hypocrisy." Until we pass through the judgment seat of Christ we cannot help but be hypocritical. That is one of the characteristics of the earthly image. Paul describes those subtle, hidden actions all of us are guilty of until we submit to the judgments of the Lord to us personally:

"Therefore thou art inexcusable, O man, whosoever thou art that judgest: for wherein thou judgest another, thou condemnest thyself; for thou that judgest doest the same things. But we are sure that the judgment of God is

according to truth against them which commit such things. And thinkest thou this, O man, that judgest them which do such things, and doest the same, that thou shalt escape the judgment of God? Or despisest thou the riches of his goodness and forbearance and longsuffering; not knowing that the goodness of God leadeth thee to repentance?"(Romans 2:1)

It is when we confess our own guilt concerning the very things we are condemning in others that the condemning spirit is taken out of our hearts. At the judgment seat of Christ we pass out of ourselves and into Him. And in Him is no condemnation. And now, being filled with the judgments of God, we deal with other people in mercy.

The Lamb of God has come to take away the sins of the world. That is, He will carry them out of the way of our relationship with God and with other people. Now, when those sins are taken out of the way, the mercy of God ministers life in relationships. Be careful that you do not unwittingly become a worker with Satan, the accuser of the brethren, who desires to bring back the sins that the Lord has carried away, and place them between you and others. James had to rebuke the brethren for doing that very thing. And what then took place? Fighting and warring among them!

VI. Approving Those Things Which Are Excellent

It is not until we are conformed to the image of God that we can approve what He approves and disapprove the same things He disapproves. We can have mercy for someone without approving what they are saying or doing. When God makes us conformable to His character, we will be faithful to that work in us. That faithfulness will express itself in our approving what God approves.

Paul speaks concerning this characteristic of the Lord that should be in us as well:

"If we suffer, we shall also reign with him: if we deny him, he also will deny us: If we believe not, yet he abideth faithful: he cannot deny himself" (2 Timothy 2:12-13).

Anytime we deny the Lord, by our words or actions, He denies us. That is, He does not put His approval on it. He does not witness to it by His Spirit. He can only witness to the truth. When Peter denied the Lord, the Lord denied Peter's denial. He did not go along with Peter's effort to deliver himself when his life was threatened. Nor will He put his approval on our similar efforts either.

Nevertheless, because He is faithful, he will abide so even in our unfaithfulness. He cannot deny what He is, and He is faithful. That characteristic of the Lord is also to be in us. The church is to be filled with faithfulness even to those who are unfaithful to the church.

The church is to be full of judgment. The church becomes full of judgment by allowing the Lord to judge us. Paul tells the Corinthians that if the church is full of judgment, (that is, of having received the Lord's judgment), and there comes in an unbeliever, the presence and word of the Lord will be so strong, the unbeliever's heart will be judged. How does such power come about in the church? By the church first submitting to the judgments of God.

If we refuse to "judge ourselves," we will be called Christians but we will think, and act, and talk like the world. This judging of ourselves is our agreeing with the Lord's witness concerning our heart condition. He is faithful in His witness.

VII. The Danger Of Delay

It is no light matter to reject the judgments of the Lord to us personally. It is a matter of life and death. The Lord came and judged Cain's envy of Abel. And in so doing, warned Cain that sin would consume him unless he, Cain, agreed with the judgment of God.

Cain rejected that judgment, when at the time, the loss was in the form of a broken relationship with his brother. But the next time God comes to deal with Cain concerning his sin, he has committed an irreversible act and has murdered Abel.

Cain's response to the new judgment of God was, "My punishment is more than I can bear." To put off the judgment of God today makes it more unbearable in the future. But more than that it causes loss, great loss, sometimes unrecoverable loss. It is because of the rejection of the judgment of God in the church, that splits, and divisions, and heartache, and infightings continue and escalate. These things ought not and need not to be.

Each member can be transformed by submitting themselves to the judgment seat of Christ. And such transformation brings the heavenly here to earth. We then, the incorruptible seed, can be taken by the Husbandman and planted by him in any situation so that fruits of righteousness might be reaped by our Lord. It is through the judgments of the Lord that what is in the head is in the body. Our salvation is contained in the judgments of the Lord.

The Righteousness Of The Law Fulfilled

I. Inward Reality

The carnal man will always look for ways to save his life. These ways are most subtle for "the heart (of carnal man) is deceitful above all things, and desperately wicked: who can know it" (Jer. 17:9)? One of these ways of the flesh is to clothe itself in outward religiosity as a substitute for inward reality. God looks upon the heart. That is to be where our attention is as well. When Moses came down from the mount and his face was reflecting the glory of God, the Israelites drew back in fear. The reason they did so was because they saw the sin of their hearts when the looked upon the glory of God on the face of Moses. When they rejected God's person, He gave them His righteousness in letter form. The Israelites became comfortable with tables of stone because they could interpret the law anyway they chose. That is why the Lord said to the Pharisees and others who handled the law:

"Well hath Isaiah prophesied of you hypocrites, as it is written, This people honoureth me with their lips, but their heart is far from me. Howbeit in vain do they worship me, teaching for doctrines the commandments of men. For laying aside the commandment of God, ye hold the tradition of men, as the washing of pots and cups: and many other such like things ye do. And he said unto them, Full well ye reject the commandment of God, that ye may keep your own tradition" (Mark 7:6-9).

Instead of the law being written on their hearts, it was perverted and misapplied out from their hearts. Those who sought after righteousness by keeping the law had the fulfillment of the law standing before them in the person of Jesus. Yet, they saw not His glory, despite always studying and trying to keep the law. Just as the Israelites rejected God's person in the Exodus, so too, did the Pharisees reject the Lord's person while he was here on earth. He did not conform to their standards of righteousness. He had no external form or comeliness that they should desire him. Trying to keep the law originates in man's ignorance, pride, and confidence in the flesh. Such efforts actually harden our heart all the more and blind us to the true glory of God.

But John the beloved writes, "And we beheld his glory, the glory as of the only begotten of the Father, full of grace and truth" (1 John 1:14). The "we" of whom John speaks were all those who saw their need of a saviour. They saw their sin and lost condition. Thus, their eyes were open to behold the glory of the Lord hidden beneath an earthly exterior.

Seeing the Lord produces life in us. The Israelites determined their own failure by their refusal to look at the sin in their hearts. They told Moses to "cover the light" that exposed such sin. The desire for a veil to be placed between the Israelites and the glory of God came out of sinful hearts turned away from God.

"Nevertheless, when it (that is, the heart) shall turn to the Lord, the veil shall be taken away" (2 Cor. 3:16).

The reason the veil was put on Moses' face was that the Israelites "prayed" him to do so. When our heart turns to God, our desire and prayer is that the veil will be taken away so that we can behold God's glory. If we attend church with a heart turned away from God, we will not be comfortable if His glory is being revealed. But if our heart is surrendered to God, we will greatly rejoice in that atmosphere. When our heart turns, we begin to see Him who is invisible. As we look upon the glory of the Lord, a change takes place in our inner being:

"But we all, with open face beholding as in a glass the glory of the Lord, are changed into the same image from glory to glory, even as by the Spirit of the Lord" (2 Cor. 3:18).

It is in beholding the glory of God and being changed that we are then able to fulfill the righteousness of the law. Seeing the righteousness of the Lord, we will "glory in heart and not in outward appearance."

"Think not that I am come to destroy the law, or the prophets: I am not come to destroy, but to fulfil" (Matt. 5:17).

The Lord's fulfillment of the law of Moses was not in letter but in Spirit. Thus, he set a much higher standard of the law than any man could interpret. That is why Paul specifies that living on a certain level fulfills the law of Christ and not the law of Moses.

"Bear ye one another's burdens, and so fulfil the law of Christ" (Gal. 6:2).

He had just finished telling the Galatians, who had been reverting to efforts of being made perfect by works of the law, that an inner heart condition created by the Spirit of God lives on a higher plane than the letter of the law.

"But the fruit of the Spirit is love, joy, peace, longsuffering, gentleness, goodness, faith, meekness, temperance: against such there is no law" (Gal. 5:22-23).

It is very evident from the teachings of Paul that no man can in and of himself keep the law. But it is also evident from Paul's writings that the righteousness of the law is to be fulfilled in and by believers. When the Lord spoke to the Pharisees, he actually gave more stringent demands than they did according to their interpretations of the law.

"Ye have heard that it was said by them of old time, Thou shalt not commit adultery: But I say unto you, That whosoever looketh on a woman to lust after her hath committed adultery with her already in his heart" (Matt. 5:27-28).

His interpretation of the law expressed the Spirit of the law. The law was the righteousness of God's person reduced to letter form. Jesus did not relate to the reduction in letter form, but to the fullness of the righteousness of God in the person of God. To so live, we must walk after the Spirit of God.

Furthermore, James tells us we are to be doers of the law:

"If ye fulfil the royal law according to the Scripture, Thou shalt love thy neighbour as thyself, ye do well . . ." (James 2:8).

And how do we fulfill the law? Will it be out of our own strength or efforts? Will it be done by listing a set of rules the members of the Church must keep? Both of these efforts will result in dismal failure. The law will only be fulfilled in us when we turn away from looking to the law and seek to be filled with and walk after the Spirit.

Some will say, "We are not under law but under grace." That is true. But if we are under grace and have received grace, we are called to a higher standard of righteousness than even the letter of the law. "To whom much is given, much is required."

The parable of the forgiven steward teaches just that. The unjust steward was forgiven a debt of huge proportion by his master. But the forgiven servant then went out and found one who owed him a pittance. When the one who owed him practically nothing asked for forgiveness, the wicked servant showed no mercy. The unjust steward (who had received grace) related to his debtor after law and not after grace. When the forgiving master was informed as to the wicked servant's behavior, he was quite "wroth" with him and treated him according to the law. The analogy is, of course, quite obvious. If we boast about receiving grace, we are then debtors to extend that same grace to others.

Peter thought he was being very generous to his brother if he forgave him seven times in a day. The Lord then told Peter, "not seven, but 70 times seven." What the Lord was saying was, "Peter, you must live in continual forgiveness of heart toward all." Such living is impossible unless we are being filled with the Spirit moment-by-moment.

"That the righteousness of the law might be fulfilled in us, who walk not after the flesh, but after the Spirit" (Rom. 8:4).

In Romans 7, Paul had just given a detailed description of his failure to keep the law. It was not the law's fault that Paul failed. He declares if any law could have given life, it was the law of God given through Moses. The problem, Paul said, was with himself: "I am carnal sold under sin." He found "no good thing in him to keep the law." But when he confessed his lack and turned to God for help, he opened himself up to receive all he needed to fulfill the law. He then presented God with a soft heart condition, the kind of heart condition that God can write His laws upon. The softer the writing surface we give the Lord, the easier the writing:

"For this is the covenant that I will make with the house of Israel after those days, saith the Lord; I will put my laws into their mind, and write them in their hearts: and I will be to them a God, and they shall be to me a people . . ." (Heb. 8:10).

When God delivered the Israelites from Eygpt, He wanted to make them a holy and peculiar people. His first desire was to write His laws upon their hearts. They, however, never gave to God the necessary writing surface, which was a soft heart. And since God could not write His law upon their hearts of stone, He wrote His law upon tables of stone. This writing did two things: it became a witness for Israel and a witness against Israel.

For those who sought after God with all their heart, the law would bring them to the same conclusion as Paul in Romans 7. The law would be their schoolmaster, teaching them about their inability to keep the law, and it would lead them to their need for a saviour (Gal. 4:1-7). Therefore, they would cry out to God for Him to forgive their sins and change their hearts.

All who truly served God in the Old Testament related to Him by faith and not after the law. That is what Paul is trying to show in Romans:

"Even as David also describeth the blessedness of the man, unto whom God imputeth righteousness without works, Saying, Blessed are they whose iniquities are forgiven, and whose sins are covered" (Rom. 4:6-7).

When we allow the Spirit of God to have His way in us, we fulfill the righteousness of the law. When we speak His words, when we follow His leading, when we do His deeds, we not only fulfill the letter of the law, we fulfill the Spirit of it.

"It was said of old time . . . But I say unto you . . . ." What the Lord said was much more exacting than what had been said of old. When we come to the Lord and confess our utter lack to live righteously before Him and confess our need for Him to live His life through us, we open ourselves to receive from Him all that God has made Jesus to be to us:

"But of him are ye in Christ Jesus, who of God is made unto us wisdom, and righteousness, and sanctification, and redemption . . ." (1 Cor. 1:30).

God has made Jesus our righteousness; He is all of these things now. He could be everybody's righteousness, but not everybody is open to receive His words, His life, His direction, His wisdom. As we open up to Him, the righteousness of Christ flows out from us. If we speak His words and do his deeds, then we can say with Paul, "It is no longer I who live, but Christ lives in me . . ." (Gal 2:20, NAS).

When we believe on Him, and while we are believing on Him, out of our belly or innermost being flow rivers of living water. These waters flow out because they first flow in. We are not the source of those waters, He is. The flow is dependent upon our opening to Him, our believing Him. If we have a soft and broken heart, we will allow the river of life to flow out of us to touch the lives of others.

II. A Dam, A Trickle, A Stream

There is now a river that flows from the throne of God. It is a life-giving river that flows without interruption. It is available to all who believe upon the Lord. David said, "The law of the Lord is perfect, converting the soul . . ." (Ps. 19:7). The word for "law" could be described as a "flow."

The flow of the Lord is perfect and complete, lacking nothing. But if we, through sin, have hardness of heart, we dam up the flow of God from coming into our hearts or from flowing out. Remember that our hearts will be hardened **through** the deceitfulness of sin. That is, when we act out our sinful desires, we move from hardness of heart to yet greater hardness. If we continually sin, our hearts are hardened more and more. We resist the flow of God, and we become a dam to the goodness of God.

But when we repent, when we confess our need, when we soften our heart, the goodness of God is then allowed to flow through us. It does not flow through us in the same measure in which it flowed in. Certainly not at first. There is too much "debris" in our hearts to allow an unrestricted flow of the goodness of God. We can liken ourselves to a funnel. The goodness of God is poured into us as in rivers at the wide end of the funnel, but our smallness of heart restricts the flow at the other end and only a trickle of His goodness may flow out from us. At least it is a start. Now the goodness of God has a breakthrough, and the uninterrupted flow into us will begin to wash away the restrictive debris in our hearts. And soon, out of our innermost beings will come streams of living water because the goodness of God has created a channel in us.

"He that believeth on me, as the scripture hath said, out of his belly shall flow rivers of living water" (John 7:38). (KJV)

If we believe on Him, **while** we believe on him, and **when** we believe of him, the rivers of living water flow out. Moment-by-moment as we believe, the flow continues.

III. The Measure We Mete

"For with what judgment ye judge, ye shall be judged: and with what measure ye mete, it shall be measured to you again" (Matt. 7:2).

It is most unfortunate that many speak about the measure in regard to financial giving. The Lord is not speaking about the measure of finances. He is speaking about the flow that comes out of us to touch the lives of other people. That which flows into us of the river of life contains in itself the desire to give to others that which we ourselves have received. There is produced in us a willingness, even an eagerness to be spent on behalf of others. With what measure we mete out our very life, to that measure it comes back to us. With what measure ye mete — the very same measure!

The "anointing" carries the flow of God out from us to others. It requires a humbling on our part to allow the river of God to flow through us to touch others. The greater the measure of that flow out from an individual, the greater the measure back to the individual.

Knitly Joined Together

"The Spirit of the Lord GOD is upon me; because the LORD hath anointed me to preach good tidings unto the meek; he hath sent me to bind up the brokenhearted, to proclaim liberty to the captives, and the opening of the prison to them that are bound . . ." (Isa. 61:1).

What is flowing out of the "anointed?" — Words of deliverance, healing, and bountifulness. And what will those who receive do toward that one who so gives?

"But I have all, and abound: I am full, having received of Epaphroditus the things which were sent from you, an odour of a sweet smell, a sacrifice acceptable, well-pleasing to God" (Phil. 4:18). The measure that flowed out of Paul and touched the Philippians came back to him in so many ways. The Philippian jailer, who along with his whole house was brought to the Lord by Paul, would have given back to Paul time and time again. Paul's sacrificial measure of giving created the same in this man and in others. Paul became the recipient of their sacrificial giving because he had first "meted out to them."

From where did Peter get his measure? From where did the other disciples receive theirs? From the Lord. And the measure that Jesus gave to them was His entire life! And what did the disciples give back? A similar measure. David tells us, "There is a river, the streams whereof make glad the city of God . . ." (Ps. 46:4). We are to be channels for that river so that the Church may be filled with joy and gladness.

It is our privilege as believers to experience the satisfaction of having the anointed flow of God go out from us to meet another's need. We must first come and "drink of the Lord" (John 7:37). That drinking is the flow of God coming into us. After drinking of the Lord, we can experience the satisfaction of "virtue going out from us."

"And Jesus said, Somebody hath touched me: for I perceive that virtue is gone out of me" (Luke 8:46).

There is to be both a flowing in and a flowing out. Our satisfaction is not fully complete until that which flows in flows out and touches others. Did not the Lord Himself say, "It is more blessed to give than to receive?" And the local Body is a place of great opportunity for us to have the river of God flow out from us to touch others.

IV. External Vs. Internal Control

The difference between trying to keep the law in our own strength vs. walking after the Spirit is quite simple. The law is for the lawless. The law is for those who do not have a nature that coincides with any given law. However, if God has given us a new nature, a nature that is like His nature, we can now keep the law without effort.

For example, the law says, "Thou shalt not bear false witness." The scribes and Pharisees, who did not have the Spirit of God in their hearts, were constantly breaking that law in regard to Jesus. They spoke of him as being a glutton and a winebibber. What were they doing? They were bearing false witness and therefore breaking the very law they seemingly so highly regarded. They witnessed to others concerning Jesus, and their witness did not tell the truth about the Lord. Wherein was the problem?

Paul tells us. "I am carnal, sold under sin" (Rom. 7:14). He further states that the law is holy, just, and good. If any law could have given life (to man), it was the law given through Moses. But we are carnal in our basic nature, which is totally contrary to the law. So when the holy and just law comes to us, the lawless in nature, we are doomed to failure in trying to keep it. Trying to keep the law will make us miserable. Trying to keep the law will cause us to become either judgmental or religious to the extreme.

The Pharisee who stood in the front of the temple misjudged the publican in the back of it. And he condemned him by extolling all his own goods works! But what he did not see, (for trying to keep the law will blind us to our own condition) is that he lived in self-justification. But the publican, who had no good works to offer God, threw himself upon the mercy of God. Our Lord says, This man (the one who asked for mercy) went down to his house justified by God. The other man left void of the approval of God for "by the works of the law, shall no flesh be justified" (Gal. 2:16). It is mercy and grace that meets the need of man, not the law. So our trying to keep the law will never restore broken humanity.

Self-justification leaves us powerless to keep the law. We live outside of God's approval, and therefore, we live in dissatisfaction. And what does a religious "keeper of the law" do while living in this place? He adds more and more laws to his list of "thou shalt not's." But there is no list of "thou salt not's" long enough to satisfy our heart. Instead of relating to God, the self-justifier relates to his list of goods works, remembering the ones he did, and trying to forget the ones he neglected to do. But all the while, he lives without the justification of God. The problem is this man is trying to control his carnal nature by a law that is totally contrary to it. As Paul says:

"Because the carnal mind is enmity against God: for it is not subject to the law of God, neither indeed can be" (Rom. 8:7).

What then is the solution? Since our old nature is contrary to the only law that could have given life, we need a new nature that can fulfill the law. God has provided that very thing for us:

"Being born again, not of corruptible seed, but of incorruptible, by the word of God, which liveth and abideth for ever" (1 Pet. 1:23).

Now we have a nature that can keep the law. But it will not be an external control. The control over the flesh (our old nature) will come from the very depths of our being as we yield to the leading of the Spirit of God:

"There is therefore now no condemnation to them which are in Christ Jesus, who walk not after the flesh, but after the Spirit. For the law of the Spirit of life in Christ Jesus hath made me free from the law of sin and death. For what the law could not do, in that it was weak through the flesh, God sending his own Son in the likeness of sinful flesh, and for sin, condemned sin in the flesh: That the righteousness of the law might be fulfilled in us, who walk not after the flesh, but after the Spirit" (Rom. 8:1-4).

When we are born of the Spirit of God, we are taken from a heart condition of "I have to keep the law" to "I **want** to keep the law." The former is a life of drudgery. The latter is a life of delight. As we yield to the Spirit's leading, we are filled with the satisfaction and strength that comes to us only through God's approval. In yielding to the Spirit, we love our "neighbor as ourselves" (and fellow Church members as well), and thus fulfill the law:

"For all the law is fulfilled in one word, even in this; Thou shalt love thy neighbour as thyself" (Gal. 5:14).

V. The Call To Glory And Virtue

"According as his divine power hath given unto us all things that pertain unto life and godliness, through the knowledge of him that hath called us to glory and virtue . . ." (2 Pet. 1:3).

Paul likens a newborn babe to a carnal individual when he tells them, "And I, brethren could not speak unto you as unto spiritual, but as unto carnal, even as unto babes in Christ" (1 Cor. 3:1). As we read Corinthians, it is obvious that their attention was on the glory associated with being used in the gifts and in having preeminence in the Church. But that is not where God's attention is. God's priority is on producing virtue in us, so that, when He glorifies us, the glory will not destroy us.

The word "virtue" means "manliness" as relating to strength. We are admonished by Paul to bear one another's burdens. But what if our strength is such that we can hardly bear our own? As we are changed into the character of Christ, we are strengthened with might in the inner man and thus able to carry what we once could not bear:

"The next day John seeth Jesus coming unto him, and saith, Behold the Lamb of God, which taketh away the sin of the world" (John 1:29)!

What glorious strength! To be able to lift up the sin of the world and take it out of the way of a relationship between God and man. How well do we do that? For example, if someone sins against us, do we allow that sin to remain as a hindrance to a relationship with that person? Or do we lift it up out of the way as if they had not sinned against us? Such lifting requires great strength.

When Joseph's brothers appeared before him, he had the power to destroy them. But God had worked virtue into Joseph and had strengthened him with might in the inner man. The glory Joseph carried as the ruler of Egypt had the virtue of God as its support. This virtue enabled him to deal with his brothers out of love by not imputing their sins to them. The Church is to be a place where we do not impute one another's sins to each other. But such action requires virtue worked into us by the Spirit of God.

We are not to choose a novice to rule in the Church because he lacks virtue . . ."Lest he be lifted up in pride!" The position of leadership requires virtue. And virtue is added to us by the grace of God and by the communion of the Lord and His Body.

"For our light affliction, which is but for a moment, worketh for us a far more exceeding and eternal weight of glory . . ." (2 Cor. 4:17).

Glory has weight to it. The greater the glory, the greater the weight. It is virtue that supports the weight of glory. If we have our attention on the glory of a position in the Church, our eyes are on the wrong thing. When we come to the place where our concern is with God producing the character of His Son in us, we are then focusing on the same thing that God is concerned with.

"For it became him, for whom are all things, and by whom are all things, in bringing many sons unto glory, to make the captain of their salvation perfect through sufferings" (Heb. 2:10).

There is an ongoing process of descent and ascent in the glory and virtue. There is a great transformation that must take place in us. God called Abraham to the glory of being the "father of many nations." But from the time he left Ur of the Chaldees until he offered Isaac on the mount, Abraham became a totally changed man. How much strength and virtue did it take for him to lift and bind Isaac, his son, upon the altar that God had required him to build?

The glory is in healing the leper; the virtue is in touching him.

The glory is on the Mount of Transfiguration; the virtue is in enduring the unbelieving people in the valley below.

The glory is in being given a name above every name; the virtue is in "first descending into the lower parts of the earth."

The glory is being "crowned with honor and glory"; the virtue is in wearing the crown of thorns.

God made the Captain of our salvation perfect through suffering. Would He take us in another way? If we are called to glory, we must answer that call by walking the path that produces the virtue of God in us as well.

"For I reckon that the sufferings of this present time are not worthy to be compared with the glory which shall be revealed in us" (Rom. 8:18).

The glory that is produced in us will reflect the virtue God has been able to work in us as we yield to Him. The Corinthians were concerned about position and power. They had their attention on the wrong things. It may be glorious to understand all mysteries, to have faith to move mountains and to speak with the tongues of angels. But if they are to be done correctly, the foundation of these things must be the virtue of love.

VI. Unto The Praise Of His Glory

"The heavens declare the glory of God . . ." (Ps. 19:1).

There is a vastness of the glory of God that we cannot even begin to imagine. All that God has done in the past, all that He is doing now, and all that He will do in the future reflects His glory! We as individuals know only a minute amount of all the wondrous works of God.

Yet, when by His workings He is able to reveal His doings to us, it will birth praise in our hearts. When the Lord does something for us, whether it be instantaneous or over a period of time, He reveals to us a bit of His glory and we cannot help but praise Him. We are created to see and to reflect His glory.

"That we should be to the praise of his glory, who first trusted in Christ" (Eph. 1:12).

This praise is birthed in us as we see His glory. When Joseph stood before Pharaoh, and later as he judged his brothers and the Word of God had come to pass in his life, his heart overflowed with praise for God. When Abraham held his newborn baby Isaac in his hands, he, too, had seen the glory of God and could not help but praise God. When David, after many years of suffering, saw the ark being brought into Jerusalem, he could not contain his praise for God.

All of these men were saying in their hearts, "This is the Lord's doing, and it is marvelous in our eyes." When David penned these words concerning the "Lord's doings," he was speaking in particular about the crucifixion of the Lord. Yet when it was being done, no one saw it as the Lord's doing—not the Roman soldiers, not the Jews, not the disciples. Later the disciples' eyes were opened to see that it was the Lord's doing, and it produced their praise unto His glory. As we believe, we will see the glory of God, and seeing it, we will be filled with praise for Him. Such praise, acquired only by faith, always produces "praise unto the glory of God." Paul speaks concerning this praise:

"When he shall come to be glorified in his saints, and to be admired in all them that believe (because our testimony among you was believed) in that day" (2 Thes. 1:10).

The word "admired" used above means to "marvel at." There are three aspects to this admiration. The first aspect is the marveling that men do who are on the outside looking in. An example can be seen in the life of Joseph. Pharaoh and Joseph's brothers both marveled at what God had done in and through Joseph. Their marveling was limited because they were on the outside looking in.

The second and third aspects are much better because the marveling is done on the "inside." When Joseph stood before Pharaoh, he was filled with an awe and admiration for what the Lord had done. His awe came from enduring the dealings of God in his life while he believed God. He had hungered for righteousness and now that hunger was being rewarded. It is true that "no flesh shall glory in God's presence." But the work of God in a man certainly shall glory in the presence of God. Joseph was filled with the praise that only comes to those in whom God has done His work.

The third aspect of marveling involves those who discern the work of God done in others because of the work of God done in themselves. When Melchizedek and Abraham left communing with one another, their hearts were filled with "praise unto the glory of God" because they were able to see the work God had done in the other. And why could they see such a work? Only because they had allowed God to do a work in them.

Such a work could never be done in someone who relates to God by keeping the law. That person will never rise above the level of flesh. That person must quit all their carnal, religious efforts and must surrender to God. They must, by faith, abandon themselves unto God and the work He wants to do in them. That work will be done in circumstances, places, and ways that will be outside of their choosing; but it will produce the virtue, the righteousness, and the glory of God that only God can produce.

Biblical Prosperity

I. In The Name Of The Lord

"Save now, I beseech thee, O LORD: O LORD, I beseech thee, send now prosperity" (Ps. 118:25).

What specifically was David praying for when he asked the Lord to send prosperity? What was David's concept of the prosperity that God would supply?

If a person who has earthly values and affections reads this verse, they think David is praying for material prosperity. But the very next verse tells us what David considered to be true prosperity:

"Blessed be he that cometh in the name of the LORD: we have blessed you out of the house of the LORD" (Ps. 118:26).

David knew from personal experience that the man or woman who came in the name of the Lord carried the blessing of God. He, himself, was that very thing to Israel when he was used by God to defeat Goliath. Did not David use the phrase, "But I come unto you in the name of the Lord of Hosts," just before killing the giant?

Biblical prosperity does not necessarily mean material prosperity. Consider Joseph: He was hated and betrayed by his brothers, sold into slavery, cast into prison, and made to suffer for a long period of time. Yet in the midst of all of these adverse circumstances, the Bible describes Joseph as a prosperous man, even though he owned absolutely nothing of this world's goods.

"And the LORD was with Joseph, and he was a prosperous man; and he was in the house of his master the Egyptian" (Gen. 39:2).

The word prosperous used here means to "push forward." It indicates that Joseph was making spiritual progress. Biblical prosperity can thus be measured in three distinct ways: by spiritual enlargement, by spiritual health and strength, and by spiritual possession.

II. Spiritual Enlargement

The Bible is very clear and descriptive concerning our narrowness and smallness when we first come to the Lord. It can be no other way. We are limited by our ignorance, lack of experiences, lack of vision, lack of spiritual fruit, prejudices, and so many other things. We are of the earth, "earthy." That condition in and of itself is not wrong. But not to recognize our smallness can cost us much time and cause much difficulty in advancing in the things of God. Recognizing our smallness makes us dependent upon God and His supply to us through the Church.

Paul had to deal with the "smallness" of the Corinthians. God had already dealt with Paul's "smallness." Remember that Paul had been a Jew of the Jews and a Pharisee of the Pharisees. Being such, he had no room in his heart for the Gentiles—probably not one! But after his conversion, God enlarged Paul's heart so that he could say,

"O ye Corinthians, our mouth is open unto you, our heart is enlarged" (2 Cor. 6:11).

"I speak not this to condemn you: for I have said before, that ye are in our hearts to die and live with you" (2 Cor. 7:3).

Can you see the enlargement of Paul's heart? He now has room in his heart to fit all these Corinthian Gentiles, and has yet more room, even for his enemies. The Corinthians, however, were too small in heart to take in the apostle. That is why he had to admonish them:

"Now for a recompense in the same, (I speak as unto my children,) be ye also enlarged" (2 Cor. 6:13).

III. Enlargement Through Distresses

"Hear me when I call, O God of my righteousness: thou hast enlarged me when I was in distress; have mercy upon me, and hear my prayer" (Ps. 4:1).

Distress in and of itself will not enlarge us. We must respond to God in the midst of our difficulties, or we will suffer in vain. The word for distress as used here means "trouble, tribulation, adversity, narrow, afflicted, and small." None of these definitions are pleasant to our flesh. But God must put us in these places if He is going to take us out of the restrictions of our carnal nature, for the carnal nature will lead us into a place of no choice! At first it will seem as if we have many options and choices in regard to the self-life. The carnal nature is deceived into thinking it already dwells in a large place. Why would it need to be enlarged? But when we walk after the flesh, we go from a broad way to a dead end. In contrast, life in the Spirit seems so restrictive at first, but if we submit to those restrictions, we will experience the power of God to bring us out into a large place:

"I called upon the LORD in distress: The LORD answered me, and set me in a large place" (Ps. 118:5).

God must come through for us in our distress. Our distress and barren condition magnify our weaknesses, of which we all have plenty. Seeing our weakness and our infirmities will cause us to look to God to make up the difference. When God makes up the difference, we are able to receive what we once did not have room for in our hearts.

We speak of "asking the Lord to come into our hearts." Have you ever considered what cramped quarters we present to Him and ask Him to endure? Yet, He is more than willing to endure these restricted living areas known as human hearts. He is confident in

His ability to change the existing conditions He finds when He first enters.

If we cooperate with the Lord's work in us, we will be enlarged to carry the blessing of God. Our prospering in Him will result in the prosperity of others. Paul speaks about glorying in his infirmities. That word "infirmities" can be described as the "inability to produce results." Such an inability causes us to look to another source for help. In such circumstances we can be enlarged because we are taken out of self-strength and made to rely upon God's strength. Our eyes are taken off of flesh as our source, instead we look for the supply to come from an infinite God.

IV. Spiritual Health And Strength

How does one measure health? The Lord came to heal us into health. Healing is the process, whereas health is the condition. Healing is progressive. Our spiritual health should always be undergoing enhancement. How do we measure health? What is to be our standard? Certainly, strength is a measure of one's health.

"For even hereunto were ye called: because Christ also suffered for us, leaving us an example, that ye should follow his steps . . ." (1 Pet. 2:21).

Peter discovered the health and strength required to follow in the steps of the Lord. At one time he believed he was up to the task. But his strength failed him. He had to be healed into the health that carries such strength.

Joseph, as he "pushed forward," exercised himself unto godliness and greater strength. Joseph went from one degree of spiritual health to yet another degree. He went from being blessed in the house of Jacob his father, to being able to endure being treated as the sinner when he had not sinned. That is not something an earthly individual can do. Such actions require the life and health of God.

John, in his epistle, writes concerning this same prosperity:

"Beloved, I wish above all things that thou mayest prosper and be in health, even as thy soul prospereth" (3 John 2).

John is not wishing but praying toward this end. Moreover, he is declaring that his prayer is being answered and that Gaius is indeed prospering. And how did John measure whether or not Gaius (or anyone else for that matter) was prospering? By seeing if they were walking in the truth!

"For I rejoiced greatly, when the brethren came and testified of the truth that is in thee, even as thou walkest in the truth" (3 John 3).

John was a man who had been used of God in many ways, including physical healings and even raising the dead. He had been on the Mount of Transfiguration, seen the Lord walk on water, and many like things. Yet he proclaims that his greatest joy from all that he had experienced in his walk with God, was to hear that his "children walked in the truth."

The Greek word for "be in health" used by John in this epistle is found most often in the writings of Paul. He always uses this word as "sound" and relates it to doctrine, words, and faith, but never to physical healing or health. In fact, this word is used by Paul when he warns Timothy that the time will come when men "shall not endure sound (be in health) doctrine. The "time" of which Paul speaks here is not the "end times." Rather, it is a time in any man's life when that man says "no" to the dealings of God.

It is the time when a man will not endure the very word of truth that would bring him into more of God's eternal life. Eternal life is a quality of life, not length of life. Jesus said, "I am come that they might have life and that more abundantly." Do you see the degrees of quality here? The words of God touch the affections of our heart. And at any time we can say, "I will not let you touch this affection—I am too fond of it." At that "time" we will cease to endure sound doctrine, and turn to those who will make us feel comfortable in our resistance to the dealings of God. We will look to have our "ears tickled."

When we come into the church setting, we bring in our imperfections and gather with others who also have imperfections. Because of the lack represented by those who gather together, there is the ever-present possibility that something will be said or done that will offend us. If we are carnal, or "sick," or weak, we will respond to those occasions out of the flesh. We will be wounded, hurt, offended. We then look to the "offender" and justify ourselves that we are in the right, and they are in the wrong. But from God's view, neither the offense nor the offender is the issue. For me (or you) God's attention is upon that which in us can be offended.

"Great peace have they which love thy law: and nothing shall offend them" (Ps. 119:165).

God is desiring to bring us to the place where nothing can offend us. Words and actions that may have once greatly disturbed us (because of inward weakness) should be dealt with, so that we live in peace, though still confronted by them. In order for us to come to that place, we must not consider the actions of others or even place blame on them in our heart. Our prayer must be, "Lord change me; I confess my lack to you."

"Looking diligently lest any man fail of the grace of God; lest any root of bitterness springing up trouble you, and thereby many be defiled . . ." *(Heb. 12:15).*

The church setting has been the place where many seeds of bitterness have been planted in people's hearts. These seeds then take root, are watered and nurtured by the flesh, and grow in depth and strength, resulting in many people being estranged from one another. One course of action many take when offended in the church is to go out from that group to seek a "better" group. The problem is that the one who leaves to go to another church takes his weakness to the next place and then the next. And he will continue to do so until the weakness is dealt with in him. Or, he may remain in the church but act out of the flesh by not speaking to others, or by warring against some, or by gossiping about the offender to others. None of these actions taken by the flesh will solve the problem. Instead, we must avail ourselves to the grace of God to minister to the lack in us.

We must confess our sin or our sickness that is the root cause of our being wounded and offended. We must see these ones who offend us as being the chastening of the Lord in our lives. And then we must make "straight paths for our feet"; that is, we must go right to the Lord with our need and respond to His direction to us so that the need in us can be met. If the need is not met, if our legs are lame as to walking in the paths of the Lord and we do not obey him, we will eventually be turned "out of the (His) way."

The sickness or weakness in our inner man is dealt with by our "making straight paths for our feet." That is, as we walk in the personal Word of the Lord for us, we find divine strength and healing flowing into our inner-being. Soon, what once offended us no longer causes us to stumble, not because the occasion of stumbling has been removed, but because our weakness has been exchanged for His strength and we can surmount what once was insurmountable to us.

When the Lord asked the many disciples who were about to forsake him, "Does this offend you?," He was trying to alert them to the lack that was inside of them. When we are offended by His words, it alerts us that we must be changed to agree with His Word. Heaven and earth will pass away, and all that does not conform to His Word, but the Word of the Lord abides forever. Jeremiah likens that Word to a hammer that breaks the rock in pieces, or to wheat, or fire. The very same Word can be any one of these three things to us depending upon our present heart condition.

If my heart is hard, then the word becomes a hammer to break down the hardness. But if my heart is hungry, that very same word can be the bread of life to feed me.

The words of the Lord bring us into divine health. But they must be endured. Many who hear the Word of God will do so at first with joy. But when the time comes in their life that the word begins to divide soul from spirit, they flee from it. In so doing, they forsake their own health. The Lord described such in the parable of the sower:

"Yet hath he not root in himself, but endureth for a while: for when tribulation or persecution ariseth because of the word, by and by he is offended" (Matt. 13:21).

This one "endureth for a while." And why does the tribulation come? Because of the word he now has heard! It is for the Word's sake. Persecution arises so that the Word can be made flesh in the hearer, but this one cannot endure. So he looks for a place that will preach another gospel that excludes persecution and tribulation to his flesh. Yet in so doing, he continues in his weakness. And he cannot follow the Lord in his paths of suffering, because the hearer has not been brought into the health that the Word intended for him to obtain. Such a one has "despised the chastening of the Lord."

V. Enduring Chastening

"For whom the Lord loveth he chasteneth, and scourgeth every son whom he receiveth. If ye endure chastening, God dealeth with you as with sons; for what son is he whom the father chasteneth not? But if ye be without chastisement, whereof all are partakers, then are ye bastards, and not sons" (Heb. 12:6-8).

Many today would reject the chastening of the Lord in their lives. Because of that, the very thing the writer to the Hebrews says, happens. "We live outside the chastening of our Father!" Because we have wiggled out from under God's dealings, and have made excuses to escape those dealings, and have substituted religious activities for those dealings, we remain unlike the Father. We bear no family resemblance. We cannot say as the Lord Himself said, "If you have seen me you have seen the Father." Why could the Son say that? Because He endured the chastening and even the scourging of the Father. And how will we come into that image? And how will we become partakers of His holiness? Only by His chastening of us done out of His heart of love!

But there is a problem we have concerning this chastening. "Now **no** chastening for the present seemeth to be joyous but grievous . . ." The writer of this epistle had experienced the chastening of the Lord. He knew the reaction it produces in the earthly man. He describes the reaction in verse 12 as "hanging-down hands and feeble knees." That is to say, when the Father deals with us to go in a certain direction, we at first, naturally respond in weakness. Yet, our healing is in pushing past the weakness we feel while enduring, through obedience, the Word our Father has spoken to us:

"Wherefore lift up the hands which hang down, and the feeble knees; And make straight paths for your feet, lest that which is lame be turned out of the way; but let it rather be healed" (Heb. 12:12-13).

Our healing is in obeying. If there is no obeying, we continue in our weakness and "sickness" or lack of health. John knew that if his children walked in the truth, they would become stronger and healthier with each advancing step. They would become partakers of the holiness of the Lord.

If we refuse chastening, we will not look like our Father. Our actions and attitudes will not reflect and glorify Him. Instead of the unity of the Spirit, we will have the chaos of carnality with its strife, envy, church splits and the like.

VI. Spiritual Possession

"But as it is written, Eye hath not seen, nor ear heard, neither have entered into the heart of man, the things which God hath prepared for them that love him" (1 Cor. 2:9).

This verse is speaking primarily of the things that God has prepared for us to partake of now, while we are here on the earth. There are things already prepared by God for you—they have your name on them. They are waiting for you at certain points of spiritual progress in your life. Abraham did not possess Isaac when first called by God. This man of faith had to follow the leading of God unto the place where that "prepared thing" was then given to him. Joseph was not placed on the throne when he first went to Egypt. He had to "push forward" to that place. David was not made king just because he was anointed to be king. Judas could have been the "apostle to the Gentiles." But another took his "bishopric" or "visitation."

"For whoso findeth me findeth life, and shall obtain favour of the LORD" (Prov. 8:35).

The word "findeth" in this verse means "come forth to" or to "appear at a certain place." Paul told the Corinthians that God calls those who are not "wise, mighty, and noble." When we are called by God, we are without these things. But where does God get his wise, mighty, and noble men and women, but from the very ones who are the "are not's." They become the "are's." And why? Because they believe God enough to do what He directs them to do. Noah is described as a man "who found grace in God's eyes." Did Noah obtain that grace by accident? No! He walked in certain paths and came forth to certain places where he was presented with the "prepared things" that God had waiting for him. God swore to Abraham that he would become the "father of many nations" after Abraham had "come forth" to the place where he was willing to offer Isaac back to God. Abraham was willing "not to spare his own son"; in so doing, he reflected the quality of character of our heavenly Father. Thus he qualified (because of his character) for the position of the "father of many nations." And God's promise, made sometime before, became Abraham's possession further down the path of spiritual progress.

"And in thy seed shall all the nations of the earth be blessed; because thou hast obeyed my voice" (Gen. 22:18).

There is a "because" involved in our possessing the things of God. The writer of Hebrews speaks of the just living by faith and by the faithfulness of God. He then goes on to say that "we are not of them who draw back unto perdition; but of them that believe to the saving of the soul" (Heb. 10:39). This phrase "saving of the soul" could be translated as "unto the soul's acquisition." That is to say, the soul now has something it did not have before. Now having it, the soul is able to administer to others what it once did not possess. The soul is enriched, prospered, blessed and able to bless.

Without enlargement, spiritual health, or spiritual possession by the individuals in the local Body, the Church lives far below what God intends. The local Body is made up of individual believers. And when these individuals come into what God intends for them to have, the Church as a whole cannot help but prosper. David said that true prosperity is "one who comes in the name of the Lord." Then he goes on to say concerning the one who comes with the blessing of God, "We have blessed you out of the house of the Lord" (Ps. 118:26).

In other words, those who are now prospering are doing so because of the prosperity of others who were able to bless and enrich them. These blessed ones recognize the source of their blessing. "We have blessed you out of the house of the Lord." They are saying, "What we have did not originate in us, but rather in God." The Lord has an abundance waiting for all who would yield to Him. It was this abundance that enabled Paul to correct the errors of the Corinthians, so that they, too, could come into the prosperity that God intended for them to have.

(6)

The True Worshippers
Of God

I. The Father's Search

"But the hour cometh, and now is, when the true worshippers shall worship the Father in spirit and in truth: for the Father seeketh such to worship him" (John 4:23).

The woman at the well had asked the Lord, "Where ought men to worship? Is there a specific geographic location?" Today many might ask, "Is there a specific denomination?" The Lord's reply discounted both geographic locations and denominations as factors in true worship. Rather, a person must have a surrendered heart that does the will of God. In order to be a worshipper of God, one must have truth in the inward man and be walking after the Spirit.

The Father's seeking of worshippers begins with His draw upon the heart of an individual. When the person being drawn begins to respond, he becomes a seeker of God. God is seeking him and he is seeking God. We cannot, however, be haphazard in our seeking:

"But without faith it is impossible to please him: for he that cometh to God must believe that he is, and that he is a rewarder of them that diligently seek him" (Heb. 11:6).

The diligent seeking of God in response to the draw upon our heart will have many expressions. One of these expressions will be the removing in ourselves of those things that can offend or stumble us. For if we turn to seek God, and as we seek Him, his light and Word will uncover much in us that is contrary to Him. These contrary things will keep us from true worship and must be removed. The diligent seeker will suffer loss others are not willing to suffer. They will allow for apparent defeat in their personal situations in order to walk "pleasing to God."

The diligent seeker is a person of faith who remembers that certain words are closely associated with believing, words such as: longsuffering, patience, overcoming, tribulation, and enduring. We are told to seek and we shall find. The Lord tells us in Revelation that He comes quickly and His reward is with Him. That is time from His viewpoint. Time from the seeker's viewpoint is more akin to the souls under the altar who question the Lord with "How long, O Lord?" Once we find and come into the possession that our seeking has produced, our viewpoint of time coincides more with the Lord's. The Lord likened this change of viewing time to a woman in travail. While in travail, time seemed like eternity. When the child was born and the pain gone, the enduring of the pain seemed like a relatively short time.

Diligent seekers are the result of the Father's draw. And the Body of Christ is used by the Spirit to draw others to Himself. When the Lord is lifted up out from our lives, by our responding to the Spirit of God, He draws all men. Not all respond to the draw, but all are drawn. The draw of God can come out of believers by their words, actions, lives, and their spirit. As we respond to the draw of God, we become the draw of God to others.

II. Worshipping In Truth

Repentance is the first act of true worship because for the first time we align ourselves with the truth. When we repent, we agree with what God is saying about our inward condition. We apply personally what God has spoken through His Son and the cross concerning the lost condition of man collectively. What God has said about mankind as a whole is, "All have sinned, and come short of the glory of God" (Rom 3:23). It is in repentance that we, for the first time, "let God be true," and that we "justify Him in His sayings" (See Romans 3:4). Let God be true and every man a liar. Let God be true in regard to what? – In regard to what he is saying about our individual heart condition.

After he had sinned with Bathsheba, David may have attempted to bring an animal to the priest as an offering to the Lord. But while he stood in line waiting his turn, his heart would have felt empty. He had spent his life relating to God by faith even though he lived during the time when the law was given preeminence. He knew the futility of offering a religious substitute for that which God really wanted. That is why he states:

"For thou desirest not sacrifice; else would I give it: thou delightest not in burnt offering. The sacrifices of God are a broken spirit: a broken and a contrite heart, O God, thou wilt not despise" (Ps. 51:16-17).

Paul, in Colossians, speaks of "will worship." Will worship originates in the individual, but true worship originates in God. False worship says, "I will worship God in this way or that way." Paul says such worship has a show of humility but it will never satisfy a truly seeking heart. (Colossians 2:18-23) David may have appeared to be very humble while standing in line waiting to offer a burnt offering to the Lord. But he knew in his heart that things were not right between God and himself. And he knew no amount of offerings would change his inward condition. Again in Psalms 51:6 David says, "Thou desirest truth in the inward parts." David knew that if he was going to be brought back into a correct relationship with God, he would have to admit the truth.

When David confessed to Nathan, "I am the man," he justified God. This justification of God brought God's justification to David. This justification of God by David opened the door for David to be blessed by God.

"Even as David also describeth the blessedness of the man, unto whom God imputeth righteousness without works, Saying, Blessed are they whose iniquities are forgiven, and whose sins are covered. Blessed is the man to whom the Lord will not impute sin" (Rom. 4:6-8).

David's justification of the Lord (i.e., agreeing with what the Spirit of God was witnessing to him) came out of a broken heart and a contrite spirit in David. When David justified God and repented, he worshipped God in spirit and in truth. God was seeking such from David all the time that this beloved man of God was estranged from him. Now the Spirit of God could flow through David to begin restoring the damage done by his actions. No amount of sacrifices or works of the law could have touched hearts wounded by David's sin. But restoration would occur as David continually yielded himself a living sacrifice unto the Lord.

How will restoration take place in the members of the Body of Christ? How will it take place out from the Body of Christ? By believers who worship God in spirit and in truth! What does God delight in? We have already seen that he does not delight in burnt offerings. And why does he not delight in those? Because God wants to restore the brokenness of humanity, and the only way that can be accomplished is through a man or woman who will do God's will.

If virtue is to flow out of us, it must first flow into us. Until we yield to God and meet Him on the common ground of truth, we dam up the flow of the goodness of God that comes to us daily.

III. The Prophet's Message

When Isaiah was first sent by God to Israel, he was given a three-fold message. The first part of his message was concerned with the condition of Israel due to its sin:

"From the sole of the foot even unto the head there is no soundness in it; but wounds, and bruises, and putrifying sores: they have not been closed, neither bound up, neither mollified with ointment" (Isa. 1:6).

The second part of the message dealt with the uselessness of traditional worship, or of worship that was outward in nature.

"To what purpose is the multitude of your sacrifices unto me? saith the LORD: I am full of the burnt offerings of rams, and the fat of fed beasts; and I delight not in the blood of bullocks, or of lambs, or of he goats" (Isa. 1:11).

Notice that God is looking for purpose in worship. Often he says, "In vain do they worship me." True worship of God brings about glorious results in changing the lives of men and women.

The third part of Isaiah's message directed them to meet together with God to have the situation resolved:

"Come now, and let us reason together, saith the LORD: though your sins be as scarlet, they shall be as white as snow; though they be red like crimson, they shall be as wool" (Isa. 1:18).

The word "reason" means "to argue to be right." At this meeting place, God argues to be right so that He may keep us from dying in our sins. If we do not submit, we shall continue walking in paths that bring destruction. But if we agree with God, let God be true, and justify God in his sayings (concerning us), then we are turned around and put on the path of life. John, in his first epistle, tells us that if we "confess our sins, God is faithful and just to forgive us our sins, and to cleanse us from our unrighteousness" (1 John 1:9). The word "confess" in this context means to "agree with what God is saying about us." This agreement touches God's faithfulness and righteousness and produces His work of cleansing us.

We are then open to receive the goodness of God. It is His goodness flowing through us that brings restoration. If the local Body of believers is filled with God's goodness, restoration will surely follow.

A broken heart and a contrite spirit, a heart surrendered to God, a person doing the will of God, will carry the anointing that brings deliverance to the captives and healing to those in need. The river of God flows through humble hearts. Every place that river touches, it brings life because it is the river of life.

IV. Worship In The Spirit

"For every high priest is ordained to offer gifts and sacrifices: wherefore it is of necessity that this man have somewhat also to offer" (Heb. 8:3).

If we are going to be priests unto God, it is of necessity that we, as the above scripture speaks of Jesus, also have "somewhat" to offer to God. Since the Lord is our example, we must look to him to see what is an acceptable offering in God's sight. We know from the Lord's words that the altar sanctifies the gift (Matt. 23:19). What altar is He speaking about?

V. The Altar Of God

When Moses was instructed to erect the tabernacle, he was told to do all things according to the heavenly pattern. Since there was one golden altar in the earthly tabernacle, it follows there is only one "golden" altar in the heavenly tabernacle "which God pitched and not man." (See Hebrews 8:5). We find that heavenly altar described in the revelation given to John by the Lord:

"And another angel came and stood at the altar, having a golden censer; and there was given unto him much incense, that he should offer it with the prayers of all saints upon the golden altar which was before the throne" (Rev. 8:3).

The true altar, however, is not a literal altar. What John saw, he saw in the spirit. The golden altar in heaven is not there for decoration. It is there for the saints of God to offer spiritual sacrifices unto the Lord. Glorious things, sacred things, most costly and precious things have been placed upon that altar. The first offering sacrificed thereon was done by God Himself. Jesus Christ is the Lamb of God "slain from the foundation of the world." And how did God offer His Son at such a time and place? How did the Son offer Himself?

"Christ, who through the eternal Spirit offered himself without spot to God, . . ." (Heb. 9:14).

And how will we offer ourselves to God? Only through the eternal Spirit! It is through a personal, living, daily sacrifice, that the knowledge of God is made known out from the believer (See Romans 12:1).

All such sacrifices out from the believer find their source in the offering of the Son by the Father upon the golden altar. Such sacrifices are done by the eternal Spirit and have divine quality.

Two things are offered upon the altar: incense and prayers. These prayers of the saints are birthed out of the work done in them by the Spirit of God. They are prayers for the will of God to be accomplished out from their lives. Our Lord himself prayed that God's will would be done in and out from Him despite his own desire for the "cup to pass from Him." The incense is that which is released in spirit out from the one who has done the will of God. An example of such a release is found in Stephen's words of forgiveness for his attackers while being stoned to death. He was to God a sweet smelling savour:

"Now thanks be unto God, which always causeth us to triumph in Christ, and maketh manifest the savour of his knowledge by us in every place. For we are unto God a sweet savour of Christ, in them that are saved, and in them that perish: To the one we are the savour of death unto death; and to the other the savour of life unto life. And who is sufficient for these things?" (2 Cor. 2:14-16)

A true, living, God-ordained sacrifice has two aspects to it. The first aspect is seen only in the natural. It is the mortifying of the flesh, resulting in death to the self-life. Those who can only see in the natural are repulsed by such actions. That is the savour of death unto death. The second aspect is seen from God's viewpoint. The mortal body has been quickened or made alive by the Spirit of God to spend itself in the will of God, and the result is life being produced in others. That is the savour of life unto life.

Gold represents the divine. The prayers and incense offered upon the golden altar represent that which is done in the believer by the Holy Spirit according to the will of God.

"But if the Spirit of him that raised up Jesus from the dead dwell in you, he that raised up Christ from the dead shall also quicken your mortal bodies by his Spirit that dwelleth in you" (Rom. 8:11).

If that same Spirit, that very same Spirit dwell in your mortal body, He will quicken you to offer yourself to the will of God for your life. We, who were dead in trespasses and sins and not able to submit ourselves to the will of God, will be made alive to obey by the eternal Spirit.

"Above when he said, Sacrifice and offering and burnt offerings and offering for sin thou wouldest not, neither hadst pleasure therein; which

are offered by the law; Then said he, Lo, I come to do thy will, O God. He taketh away the first, that he may establish the second" (Heb. 10:8-9).

He takes away the first, that is, our trying to serve God out of the works of the law, and He establishes the second in men, which is worshipping God in spirit and in truth.

VI. Partaking Of The Altar Of God

"We have an altar, whereof they have no right to eat which serve the tabernacle" (Heb. 13:10).

It is this divine altar of which we have the "right to partake, whereof those who serve the (earthly) tabernacle do not." The word "right" in this verse means "capacity, power, authority, liberty, strength, and/or competency." We all partake of it to differing degrees. To whatever extent we have offered ourselves to God upon that altar, that will be the extent to which we are able to partake of it.

Abraham gives a striking example of this truth. When God first appeared to Abraham after he went into Canaan land, Abraham built an altar (Gen. 12:7). Our willingness to build altars comes out of God's grace to us. Abraham then put something upon the altar. Until God "graced" Abraham, he had put nothing upon the altar. But the eternal Spirit worked in Abraham and soon he was offering his natural life and all its affections upon the altar of God. This offering of himself to God enabled him to be changed. That change enabled him to receive the things of the Spirit of God.

"The natural man receiveth not!" There must be a change in us. That change is brought about by our cooperating with the work of God in us. We offer up spiritual sacrifices to God by giving of ourselves to fulfill His will. Such worship brings life to others. Even today, we are partakers of the altars that Abraham built. The blessing of Abraham comes upon all who believe. So too, as we sacrifice ourselves upon the altar of God, we are blessed and able to bless. It is our privilege to offer something back to God who has given His all to us.

The more the "I" in us decreases, the more our capacity to partake of the altar of God increases. When we offer ourselves to God, such offerings are put upon the "golden altar." Think of the awesome privilege we have to put "somewhat" upon that altar. Think of the offerings that have been placed by the Lord's Church upon that altar—glorious and sacred offerings. Many have put all upon that altar, holding nothing back, that they might do the will of God for their lives. A martyr is one who has put even their last breath upon that altar.

VII. No Substitute

"And if thou wilt make me an altar of stone, thou shalt not build it of hewn stone: for if thou lift up thy tool upon it, thou hast polluted it" (Ex. 20:25).

We are not to "lift up our tool upon the altar." That is, we are not to diminish or add to that which God is asking from us. If our offering brings pain to others (and it often will), we are to follow through in obedience to God. We must give to God that which He requires. To give Him a substitute is to pollute the altar. The Lord has great purpose in that which he specifies as an offering. We may not understand it, or see His end in the matter, but we are to obey fully. If God were to call us to the mission field, no amount of our financial giving to missions would substitute for our actual going. To obey is better than sacrifice. We receive the full approval of God in our hearts when we completely conform to His commands.

Faith gives to God today that which becomes the foundation for God's work tomorrow. We do not understand how God is going to use that which He is requiring. We walk by faith, not by sight.

Cain sensed that Abel carried in his heart the approbation of God. The Spirit of God witnessed through Abel to Cain. But Cain wanted the approval of God upon his sacrifice without giving God what God wanted. God's reply to Cain was, "If thou doest well, shalt thou not be accepted" (Gen. 4:7)? That is, "Cain, you will receive My approval in your heart if you give Me what I am asking from you. But do not expect My approval on a substitute for it." Sin conquered Cain because he did not give God that which the Lord was requiring.

Knitly Joined Together

We do not understand why God might ask for a particular thing. But we can be sure that if God is asking for it, there is an advantage to us (perhaps much further along the way) if we give God what He wants. Our spiritual progress may depend totally upon our giving the right sacrifice to the Lord.

"O send out thy light and thy truth: let them lead me; let them bring me unto thy holy hill, and to thy tabernacles. Then will I go unto the altar of God, unto God my exceeding joy: yea, upon the harp will I praise thee, O God my God" (Ps. 43:3-4).

Without truth, we will never come to the altar of God. We may make sacrifices, but they will all be in vain. They will be what the Word calls "vain worship." David knew without God's light and God's truth, he would not be able to properly approach the altar of God.

If we are going to partake of the golden altar of God, then we must put ourselves on it. The more of ourselves we put on it, the greater our capacity is to partake of that altar. That is why Abraham recognized Melchizedek as being from God. He not only recognized Melchizedek as being from God, but he highly valued this man. He opened himself up to receive what this priest of God would impart to him.

When Melchizedek greeted Abraham, he did so in this way:

"And he blessed him, and said, Blessed be Abram of the most high God, possessor of heaven and earth . . ." (Gen. 14:19).

When he blessed Abraham, Abraham received something in his inner man. He left Melchizedek with more than when he first met him. Their communion resulted in Abraham being fed by a man who, at this point, had made a greater commitment to God than even Abraham. We see the evidence of this blessing of Abraham by Melchizedek when Abraham answered the king of Sodom:

"And Abram said to the king of Sodom, I have lift up mine hand unto the LORD, the most high God, the possessor of heaven and earth. That I will not take from a thread even to a shoelatchet, and that I will not take any thing that is thine, lest thou shouldest say, I have made Abram rich . . ." (Gen. 14:22-23).

Where did Abraham get the strength to reject the offer of the king of Sodom? Notice carefully his words in verse 22. How does he describe the Lord? — as "the most high God, the possessor of heaven and earth!" He had never so spoken of God until after his meeting with Melchizedek. But that is exactly the description Melchizedek used of God when he greets Abraham. Abraham's revelation of God increased because of his meeting with the priest of the Most High God. These two men were knit together because of the offering of themselves (through the eternal Spirit) upon the golden altar of God.

In his poem regarding suffering, H. E. Hamilton King offered these thoughts:

> . . . If he should call thee from thy cross today,
> Saying, It is finished! — that hard cross of thine
> From which thou prayest for deliverance,
> Thinkest thou not some passion of regret
> Would overcome thee? Thou would say, "So soon?
> Let me go back and suffer yet awhile
> More patiently; — I have not yet praised God!"

Have we yet praised God: What of ours has been put upon the golden altar of God in obedience to and love for Him? Have we so obeyed God only to have others reject us, scorn us, misjudge and even hate us? Then rejoice greatly, for all of that mistreatment gives you something more to offer to God. The Lord hid not his face from shame and spitting. He place it upon the altar and continued toward his persecutors with love and longsuffering.

Why would strife and division exist in a church? It is because the self-life has not been placed upon the altar. If the church is going to offer to God that which glorifies Him, the members of the local Body must go through a purification process.

"But who may abide the day of his coming? and who shall stand when he appeareth? for he is like a refiner's fire, and like fullers' soap: And he shall sit as a refiner and purifier of silver: and he shall purify the sons of Levi, and purge them as gold and silver, that they may offer unto the LORD an offering in righteousness" (Mal. 3:2-3).

Offerings of righteousness follow purification. The Lord desires to cleanse His temple.

VIII. The Temple Of The Lord

Where does worship take place? In the temple! Paul questioned the Corinthians:

"Know ye not that ye are the temple of God, and that the Spirit of God dwelleth in you" (1 Cor. 3:16)? Peter adds: "Ye also, as lively stones, are built up a spiritual house, a holy priesthood, to offer up spiritual sacrifices, acceptable to God by Jesus Christ" (1 Pet. 2:5).

These spiritual sacrifices have the purpose of bringing life to others. These sacrifices find their expression out from our mortal body. As we yield ourselves to the Spirit of God, men see our good works and "glorify our Father in heaven." Romans 12:1 tells us we are to "offer our bodies a living sacrifice which is our reasonable service." The word "service" in this verse means "worship." When we yield to the Spirit of God, when we pay the price in the natural realm in order to express the Spirit of God, that is true worship. It is "reasonable" to offer ourselves wholly unto the Lord, since He offered Himself wholly unto us.

"Wherefore, when he cometh into the world, he saith, Sacrifice and offering thou wouldest not, but a body hast thou prepared me . . ." (Heb. 10:5).

God has given us a medium of worship. We express worship out from our mortal body. The things we suffer while doing the will of God become our sacrifice to the Lord.

We sing, "We bring the sacrifice of praise into the house of the Lord." Perhaps a more accurate song would be "We bring the sacrifice that produces praise into the house of the Lord." For surely, as we yield ourselves in obedience to God, we will see His glory, and praise will be birthed in our hearts. But without this "living sacrifice," we will be blinded to the Lord's doings. They will not be "marvelous in our eyes," and we will be without. Being without, we will not be able to bless others. Paul admonished the Corinthians, "As the Lord has prospered you, you prosper others." It can be no other way, and as we "present our bodies a living sacrifice," the Lord's prosperity will overflow us. Our being a living sacrifice and its subsequent prosperity is the basis of our communion with the Lord.

IX. The Joy Of The Lord

The joy of the Lord belongs first to Him, and then He shares it with us. "Well done, thou good and faithful servant . . . enter thou into the joy of thy lord" (Matt. 25:21). Here, the servant's faithfulness was the reason for the master's joy. It was a faithfulness that took place in the midst of circumstances that tended to unfaithfulness. The master went far away. He was gone a long time. The environment was hostile to these servants. Nevertheless, they remained faithful and brought joy to their lord. His words of approval then filled them with joy.

When reading the New Testament, notice how often the joy of the Lord is in the midst of unpleasant circumstances to the flesh. The joy of the Lord is not based upon circumstances; it rules over negative situations. When we spend ourselves to do the will of God, we are increasing our capacity to share in the joy of the Lord.

Paul lists some of the that things he suffered while doing the will of God. These included: shipwreck, fastings, hungers, beatings and the like. But out from his sacrifice came the churches at Corinth, and Galatia, and Philippi, to name a few. In any given service, Paul would sit and listen to the testimonies of those who were brought to the Lord because of his sacrifices. The Spirit of God would speak to him, "Well done, thou good and faithful servant; enter thou into the joy of thy Lord." In the depths of Paul's being, and because of the tremendous price he paid in the natural, he could truly enter into the joy of the Lord.

Yes, the newborn babes in Christ in these churches would be elated by what the Lord had done for them and rightfully so. But they did not know about the depth of joy carried by the apostle—joy that was the result of his faithfulness and sacrifice.

Paul truly "brought the sacrifice of praise into the house of the Lord." It showed in his beaten back, the bruised body from stonings, the loss of his natural advantages of being a Jew of the Jews.

"Looking unto Jesus the author and finisher of our faith; who for the joy that was set before him endured the cross, despising the shame, and is set

down at the right hand of the throne of God" (Heb. 12:2).

The joy spoken of here was and is partaken of by God the Father, the Son Himself, and all those who would be brought to God by the "travail of his soul" (Isa. 53:11). It was a joy that was set before Jesus, the son of man. He did not possess it before the cross. He had to endure in order to obtain it. So too, when we endure in the will of God, we will obtain that which we did not have before such endurance.

The joy of the Lord for the servant followed faithfulness. The Lord's joy followed the travail of His soul. Paul's joy was the Christians in all the churches the Lord used him to begin. True worship will bring restoration in others through the worshipper and will fill that one with the joy of the Lord. "The Father seeketh such!"

Let Us
Keep The Feast

I. Lifeless Traditions

"Therefore let us keep the feast, not with old leaven, neither with the leaven of malice and wickedness; but with the unleavened bread of sincerity and truth" (1 Cor. 5:8).

The feast of which Paul speaks is the communion of the saints. It is sometimes very difficult for us to see outside our traditional concepts when we read the Bible. For example, when reading of communion, we may relate all of the Scriptural context to the outward symbols of bread and wine. But that is really all the bread and wine are: outward symbols which represent spiritual truths.

Tradition is an outward pattern taken from something that once had the life of God in it. And we can participate in the outward form over and over again without it ministering life to us because God is not in the outward form. He may have been at one time, and we were greatly blessed by Him in it. But He is no longer in that form, yet we continue holding on to it.

Partaking of the communion elements in and of themselves never communicates the life of God to our inner man. Always keep in mind that the words the Lord spoke were Spirit and life. They were intended to minister to our inner man. Outward forms cannot do that, only the Spirit and life of God can.

The Corinthian Church was involved in the outward form of communion, but they were not being increased because of it:

"Now in this that I declare unto you I praise you not, that ye come together not for the better, but for the worse" (1 Cor. 11:17).

II. True Communion

Consider the situation at Corinth through the eyes of the apostle Paul. When the Corinthians gathered together, they came from a place of self-seeking. Many were in sin. Many had been careless all week as to the things of God. Many carried bitterness, envy, and strife. They brought divisions into the church which, of course, would destroy true communion. Of how many of them could it have been said, "Blessed is he who comes in the name of the Lord?" How many had been prospered in spirit by time spent with God? How many had fed upon the life and Spirit of God at home during the week so that they would have to give to one another? How many had given themselves for one another in such a way as to put others in remembrance of the Lord?

"And when he had given thanks, he brake it, and said, Take, eat; this is my body, which is broken for you: this do in remembrance of me" (1 Cor. 11:24).

At the time the Lord spoke these words concerning the bread and wine, the disciples did not understand what He was saying to them about communion. They were not feeding upon Him, they were feeding upon their own ambitions and desires. Their actions and words and attitudes were quite unlike His. During this solemn feast they debated among themselves as to who would be the greatest. And when they left that communion service, they went out, not for the better, but for the worse. They were weak and sick, and that weakness was reflected in many ways.

It was seen in Peter and in the others when they said they would all "die for the Lord." They were unaware of their spiritual condition. Their weakness was seen in their denying Him. Yet one disciple, John, who was in communion with the Lord, received enough life from the Lord to be present at the cross.

The apostles had previously heard the Lord say these other mystical words concerning true communion:

"Verily, verily, I say unto you, Except ye eat the flesh of the Son of man, and drink his blood, ye have no life in you" (John 6:53).

They did not understand it any better than those disciples who "went back and walked no more with the Lord." However, something kept the apostles following Him despite their lack of understanding. And yet their lack prevented them from feeding upon His life and Spirit to obtain needed strength.

We too, like the Corinthians and the disciples before them, can miss the life that God has for us to share with others by our neglecting personal communion with Him. We too, can come through the church doors and bring in attitudes and sin that would have been corrected had we truly supped with the Lord. Our lack of feeding upon Him causes the feast to be contaminated with the leaven of malice and wickedness.

We must realize that if just one person brings such into the service, the communion is tainted to some degree. "A little leaven leaveneth the whole lump" (Gal. 5:9). One cannot make a loaf of bread and put a certain seasoning in one end of the bread and not the other. The flavor goes throughout the loaf. "We being many are one bread." And being such causes a "little leaven to leaven the whole lump."

The apostle Paul admonishes us to "purge out the old leaven of malice and wickedness." Each individual must examine himself to see if these things are present in his heart. Then each member must so feed upon the Lord that he is filled with sincerity and truth. Personal communion with the Lord is to be the basis of the communion of the saints.

"Therefore let us keep the feast, not with old leaven, neither with the leaven of malice and wickedness; but with the unleavened bread of sincerity and truth" (1 Cor. 5:8).

Knitly Joined Together

When the Lord said, "Take and eat" to His disciples, he offered them only sincerity and truth. His life was free from malice and wickedness. To feed upon His life was to feed upon sincerity and truth. When the disciples offered their words to one another at the Last Supper, they offered one another malice, ambition, and striving. As they fed upon each other's words, it only made them weaker than before. They came together that night of nights in the first "communion service," not for the better but for the worse.

True communion is a feast of the life of God passing from one saint to another resulting in increase in the Body. Consider the many forms of blessing this communion is to take. We are told to "love one another, serve one another, edify one another, comfort one another, exhort one another, provoke one another unto good works, admonish one another, and prefer one another in honor." What a spiritual feast takes place when people come into the service in humility and meekness.

The Spirit of God can then flow from one member to another, blessing, enriching, and strengthening the Body. Then when we go out from the meeting, we have come together for the better. Some give, others receive; some feed, others eat; some bless, others are blessed; but all are increased in God.

Melchizedek, when sent by God to meet Abraham, brought forth bread and wine, the symbols of communion. In the Spirit, life went out of Melchizedek and strengthened Abraham. Abraham's revelation of God was increased by "his coming together" with Melchizedek. When they left their communing together in the Spirit, both of these men were blessed and strengthened. Melchizedek walked away with the full feeling that comes from giving someone the life that God has shared with them. There were not many people with whom Melchizedek could share his "pearls." He hungered to feed others just as our Lord did while on earth. How satisfying it was when he could do just that. Jesus ate by feeding. His meat was to do the will of the Father. So too, Melchizedek, and all those who are increased by God, eat by feeding. That is their portion in the communion of the Lord and the fellowship of the saints.

Others, like Abraham, eat by feeding on the life of God in those made living bread by the work of God. Abraham left the meeting with Melchizedek and rejoiced in spirit that his hunger for God had just been ministered to by another member of the body.

III. Preparation

We must spend time alone with the Lord to prepare our hearts for communion with the saints. This preparation includes "tarrying one for another." That is, we must look to the Lord to have something to give to a brother or sister in need. It is a common thing, and very detrimental, for the Church as a whole to make a distinction between "clergy and laity." If we make that distinction in our hearts, we will neglect going before the Lord during the week. The burden of the entire service then falls upon the minister. That is not the intention of God. Every joint is to supply. That supply can take the form of gifts of the Spirit, a word or testimony, a prayer, a song, a hunger, an expectancy, or many other things. But we are all to come with something in our hearts for the "communion service."

We are to have judged ourselves so that we are free from malice and wickedness. We cannot judge ourselves without the aid of the Spirit of God. We are to pray as David did, "Search me, O God, and know my heart: . . . and see if there be any wicked way in me . . ." (Ps. 139:23-24). Such judgment will cause a cleanness to exist in the gathering of the believers. As Paul describes the condition of the Corinthians, it was obvious they were neglecting to go before the Lord with such a prayer. And because of this neglect, many things were brought into the service that destroyed true fellowship with one another and greatly hindered the moving of the Spirit. It should be able to be said of each believer who enters the meeting, "Blessed is he who comes in the name of the Lord."

To be properly prepared is to exclude certain things from our lives:

"Ye cannot drink the cup of the Lord, and the cup of devils: ye cannot be partakers of the Lord's table, and of the table of devils" (1 Cor. 10:21).

When James rebuked the group to which he was writing, he told them their wisdom was not from above, but was earthly, sensual, and devilish. They had taken the methods of this world, as well as its wisdom, and brought it into the Church. They made themselves "friends" with the world by using the world's methods and ambitions in the Church. In so doing, they opposed what God was wanting to do in their midst. Before these "brethren" came together with one another, they would "feed" on this world in their hearts. They would partake of the cup of devils. That cup contains certain things such as envy, strife, backbiting, murder, and the like. That is why James rebuked them for warring and killing one another. Paul had to warn the Galatians not to "bite and devour one another."

For example, it is not unlikely that an individual could feed all week long on some wrong (real or imagined) done against them by another brother or sister. The feeding upon this wrong festers and increases bitterness and isolation in the individual. How then could this one "keep the feast" correctly?

The cup of the Lord is filled with life. In contrast, the cup of devils is filled with death. The Lord's cup is a cup of blessing. If one is battling unforgiveness toward another, he can "eat at home" by feeding upon the Lord's forgiveness and grace. Being cleansed and strengthened, he can then keep the feast with the unleavened bread of sincerity and truth.

"Wherefore whosoever shall eat this bread, and drink this cup of the Lord, unworthily, shall be guilty of the body and blood of the Lord" (1 Cor. 11:27).

If we do not properly value the life the Lord has given for us, we will neglect all the benefits of it. We will spend our time feeding upon other things, to our spiritual detriment. "Except we eat his flesh and drink his blood, we have no life in us." In setting aside our personal feeding upon Him, we deem His life to be worth less than other things. If we do not feed upon the life of the Lord, we will not have the strength to walk in paths of blessing. We will walk out of the way and bring ourselves to places of judgment and correction.

Peter ate the "bread" of the Lord unworthily when he rejected the Lord's words to him concerning his pending denial of the Lord. In so doing, Peter became unable to fulfill his heart's desire to follow the Lord unto death. And he found himself in a place of defeat and of chastening by the Lord:

"For he that eateth and drinketh unworthily, eateth and drinketh damnation (judgment) to himself, not discerning the Lord's body" (1 Cor. 11:29).

"But when we are judged, we are chastened of the Lord, that we should not be condemned with the world" (1 Cor. 11:32).

The next time we see Peter and the Lord supping, Peter is wide open to eat that which the Lord wants to feed him. Now he is "eating the bread" worthily. It is in the proper place in his heart. Soon he is strengthened with might in the inner man to such a degree that he can stand against those from whom he once fled.

IV. Abide

"Abide in me, and I in you. As the branch cannot bear fruit of itself, except it abide in the vine; no more can ye, except ye abide in me" (John 15:4).

Without abiding in the Lord, it is impossible for us to bring forth the fruit that makes the wine of the communion service.

"But I say unto you, I will not drink henceforth of this fruit of the vine, until that day when I drink it new with you in my Father's kingdom" (Matt. 26:29).

Was our Lord talking about drinking literal grape juice or wine after His resurrection? Of course not! He was speaking of the fruit that would be produced out from the lives of disciples who would bring forth fruit by abiding in Him.

The Lord has a very definite appetite and thirst. While being crucified he cried, "I thirst." It was and still is a thirst for the wine of the fruit of those who abide in Him. We, who carry the Lord's Spirit, also have this appetite and thirst in us. The communion of the saints and of the Lord Himself is what satisfies these desires.

Unless we abide in Him, we cannot bring forth this fruit. How do we abide? John, in his first epistle is very clear on this matter.

"And he that keepeth his commandments dwelleth (abideth) in him, and he in him. And hereby we know that he abideth in us, by the Spirit which he hath given us" (1 John 3:24).

Knitly Joined Together

When David extolled the goodness of God, he spoke of the benefits of the Lord's testimonies, statues, law, and commands (Ps. 19) Then in verse 11, he declares:

"Moreover by them is thy servant warned: and in keeping of them there is great reward" (Ps. 19:11).

We oftentimes do not keep the Lord's commands because we are unaware of the great reward contained in doing so. In the keeping of them, that is, even while they are being kept, there is great reward. The reward includes receiving the Spirit of God. "He gives the Spirit to those who obey him" (Acts 5:32). By keeping the directives of the Lord, we obtain the peace and rest and approval of God — great reward indeed. But many times our attention is drawn elsewhere and we are neglectful to abide by keeping the Lord's Word to us.

The enemy of our soul cannot tolerate an individual who has determined to abide in God, and for good reason on his part. For that individual who abides in God becomes insulated from all the enemy's tactics:

"We know that whosoever is born of God sinneth not; but he that is begotten of God keepeth himself, and that wicked one toucheth him not" (1 John 5:18).

The word for "toucheth him not" means does "not attach himself to." No wonder the wicked one will do all he can to keep a believer from abiding in the Lord. If we do not abide, we get outside our area of complete protection. Then the wicked one gets on our back and stays there, drawing all of our strength out of us. We then have nothing to offer to anyone else. Our only recourse to "getting him off our back" is to run into the Lord. As we submit to God and resist the devil, he will flee from us.

There are obvious signs to our abiding: rest, peace, and a great awareness of the Lord. And there are obvious signs of our not abiding: anger, unrest, strife, and self-seeking.

Our abiding brings a full confession that Jesus is the Son of God:

"Whosoever shall confess that Jesus is the Son of God, God dwelleth in him, and he in God" (1 John 4:15).

This confession is not in word only. The confession must have three elements in it as described by John in chapter 5. These elements are: the water, the blood, and the Spirit. That is how Jesus came. His Word agreed with the Spirit of God and His life (the blood) expressed both the Word and the Spirit. For our confession to be complete, there must be agreement between our words, our spirit, and our actions. That agreement is necessary for a true and complete confession.

It takes a very determined effort to abide in the Lord. It is a moment-by-moment thing, for at any time something may come to tempt us out of our abiding place. Paul spoke of his life being an exercise to always keep his conscience clear of offense toward God and toward man (Acts 24:16).

"And now, little children, abide in him; that, when he shall appear, we may have confidence, and not be ashamed before him at his coming" (1 John 2:28).

The word "now" is very appropriate. When is now? It is now. Five minutes from now it will still be now. We live in the now. Now, little children abide in Him. John does not have to tell the fathers to abide in Him. That would be their manner of life. The little children would have a tendency to wander out from Him. Abiding in Him is what causes us to mature to being a father. We grow up in Him and only in Him.

When the Lord said, "All shall know me from the least even to the greatest," He was speaking of time spent abiding in Him. Those who abide in Him go from being the least to becoming the greatest. In Him is our place of increase.

John tells us that while we abide in Him, our "love is made perfect." When we abide in Him, we do not sin. We hit the mark (God's mark) as to our words, attitude, and spirit. As we abide in Him, we reflect Him so that "as He is, so are we in this world." Such a reflection causes great comfort and boldness. It takes us out of torment.

John is very specific concerning the qualifications for abiding. He tells us that in God is no darkness and no sin. We cannot take our darkness or sin into God. That is why John gives us the encouraging exhortation concerning our sin:

"If we confess our sins, he is faithful and just to forgive us our sins, and to cleanse us from all unrighteousness" (1 John 1:9).

Being cleansed, we can enter into and abide in God. John is also very clear on what constitutes darkness. "He that hateth his brother is in darkness . . ." (1 John 2:11). David asked the Lord a question concerning abiding in God:

"LORD, who shall abide in thy tabernacle? who shall dwell in thy holy hill?" (Ps. 15:1)

Another version words this question, "Lord, who shall be a guest in your tent?" Do you desire to be God's "guest"? God was gracious to David and answered his question. Certain qualifications must be met. These qualifications include: "having clean hands and a pure heart, walking uprightly, and speaking the truth in one's heart." They also include "not backbiting with the tongue, or bearing false witness against another."

Grace is not an excuse to eliminate these qualifications from abiding in the Lord. Be very careful concerning this point. In Him is no sin, no darkness! And we are not going to slip by and enter into Him with sin and darkness. Cain tried to do so. And John takes us right back to Cain's actions and attitudes in his epistle, thus making that Old Testament truth, New Testament truth.

"Not as Cain, who was of that wicked one, and slew his brother. And wherefore slew he him? Because his own works were evil, and his brother's righteous" (1 John 3:12).

Cain was the first of the "false brethren." He was the physical brother of Abel, but he was false in that relationship. He did not act "brotherly" toward his brother. Why? Because he lived in darkness while Abel lived in the light.

God so loved the world that He gave us His Son. His Son did not come to condemn the world. There was no condemnation coming out of the Lord's heart toward the people. But, people's rejection of the Lord caused their hearts to be filled with condemnation.

Darkness always feels condemned when it rejects the light. Cain felt condemned around Abel. But Abel was not condemning him, Cain's own heart was condemning him.

God told Cain, "If thou doest well, thou shalt be accepted." Cain could have been a guest in God's tent, but he did not meet the qualifications. John warns us not to be deceived. "He that doeth righteousness is righteous."

False brethren (those who act falsely toward the other brethren) contaminate the communion of the saints. They walk in hatred, and we have already seen that John equates hatred with darkness.

"Whosoever hateth his brother is a murderer: and ye know that no murderer hath eternal life abiding in him" (1 John 3:15).

As stated before, eternal life is a quality rather than a quantity. If hatred is in our heart in the form of envy, bitterness, unforgiveness and the like, we do not have the quality of the life of God. The Lord has come to give us that quality of life.

"And this is the promise that he hath promised us, even eternal life" (1 John 2:25).

The very first verse of John's epistle speaks of that which was "from the beginning." That which was from the beginning was the life in and of God, eternal life. Even though man sinned and rebelled against God and entered into death, eternal life was still available in God. Noah partook of it. So too, did Abraham, David, Joseph, and so many more. Jesus came to manifest that life in flesh. The Word and the life became flesh. As we are filled with eternal life, we are able to feed one another.

False brethren are those like Ishmael who are of the flesh and persecute those who walk after the Spirit. David had to contend with such:

"My soul is among lions: and I lie even among them that are set on fire, even the sons of men, whose teeth are spears and arrows, and their tongue a sharp sword" (Ps. 57:4).

Who set these ones on fire against David? Other false brethren.

And James rebuked similar brethren's actions when he told them that such actions are "set on fire of hell." What followed? They warred against one another and "killed one another." Bearing false witness against another will "kill" that person in the heart of the hearer of the false witness unless the hearer is abiding in the Lord and in life. We can know truth about another and still bear false witness about them. Aren't you glad God is not a busybody? That instead of exposing sins, His love covers a multitude of them?

We will abide in Him if we "keep his commandments" and if we "confess that Jesus is the Son of God." We will know that we are abiding in Him because we love the brethren. And we will know we have passed out of death and into life by our willingness to sacrifice ourselves for the benefit of others. All who abide in God abide in life. All who abide in God, love.

It is in constant abiding that we bring forth fruit. This fruit is the fruit of the vine our Lord partakes of now in His kingdom. It is the true wine of the communion of the saints. He does in us, yet again, His first miracle. He changes the water (His Word in us) into wine (fruitfulness of His Word).

V. In Remembrance Of Me

It is through the communion of the saints that we as individuals are ministered to and brought to a place of being able to minister. The Body is to contain healing, restoration, correction, and strengthening for those who have newly come to the Lord. As time goes on, and we are ministered to, we then become able to minister. Our first order in the communion of the Lord is to receive:

"For who maketh thee to differ from another? and what hast thou that thou didst not receive? now if thou didst receive it, why dost thou glory, as if thou hadst not received it" (1 Cor. 4:7).

This receiving should always cause us to walk in humility and appreciation for the Body of Christ; all the while realizing that ministry to us. At the same time, we should realize there is a greater depth of communion that awaits us within the Body and with the Lord as we go on with Him.

The life of God is ministered to us so that others might come into that same life. The life of God will bring us to a certain deliverance:

"For we which live are always delivered unto death for Jesus' sake, that the life also of Jesus might be made manifest in our mortal flesh" (2 Cor. 4:11).

We are delivered "**to** death" so that others might be delivered "**from** death." Only those who are alive in the Lord can be "delivered unto death." It is the life of God in them that allows them to be delivered to such a place.

"Forasmuch then as the children are partakers of flesh and blood, he also himself likewise took part of the same; that through death he might destroy him that had the power of death, that is, the devil; And deliver them who through fear of death were all their lifetime subject to bondage" (Heb. 2:14-15).

It was in death that the life of Jesus was made manifest in its fullness. It was His life that enable Him to reject deliverance from the cross. He would have us "show forth His death til He comes." But in order to do that, we must first be partakers of His life.

Again David declares that the law (or flow) of the Lord is perfect. The benefits of abiding in God include: our souls being converted and restored, our eyes being enlightened, our being given the wisdom of God, and our being purified (See Psalms 19:7-11).

Having been restored, we are able to overcome the sin and death from others that is directed against us. We become workers together with God. God so loved the world, He gave His son. In order for the Son to be a worker with God, He had to have His heart free from condemnation. Instead of condemning man, He came to feed them. He is the true Bread sent down from heaven. Condemnation will never meet the need of the human heart. Only the Bread of Life will.

"That I may know him, and the power of his resurrection, and the fellowship of his sufferings, being made conformable unto his death . . ." (Phil. 3:10).

The partaking of the power of His resurrection precedes our

fellowshipping with Him in His sufferings. That resurrection life so often comes to us through the communion of the saints. True communion will result in strength and health. It will aid us in our maturing in the Lord. It will fill us with life. Being alive with the life of God, we will then be willing to be led where we once feared to go. We will allow God to "deliver us unto death so that others may live."

"As it is written, For thy sake we are killed all the day long; we are accounted as sheep for the slaughter" (Rom. 8:36).

Paul quoted Isaiah in the earlier part of Romans and said, "All we like sheep have gone astray," but now we have been brought back into the sheepfold, cared for, nursed, restored, and matured.

We have been brought to a place of preparedness, whereby we can enter a deeper level of communion, "The fellowship of his sufferings."

"Always bearing about in the body the dying of the Lord Jesus, that the life also of Jesus might be made manifest in our body. For we which live are alway delivered unto death for Jesus' sake, that the life also of Jesus might be made manifest in our mortal flesh. So then death worketh in us, but life in you" (2 Cor. 4:10-12).

Why would Paul allow death to work in him? Because he was living in the power of the Lord's resurrection life. So living, he could put others in "remembrance of the Lord's death." We too will be able to remind others of the Lord's death as it is lived out in us. John the beloved, as did Paul, so lived:

"That which was from the beginning, which we have heard, which we have seen with our eyes, which we have looked upon, and our hands have handled, of the Word of life; (For the life was manifested, and we have seen it, and bear witness, and show unto you that eternal life, which was with the Father, and was manifested unto us;) . . ." (1 John 1:1-2).

John saw and experienced it. Thus he could say, "We have seen it, and bear witness, and **show it unto you!**" Herein is one of the great purposes of the communion of the saints: to bring us to a place where we are so full of the life of God that we "can show forth the Lord's death til he comes."

To the natural man, death is to be feared because it is the end. But to the spiritual man, death is the place wherein the life of God is released to a greater degree than ever before.

If we do not have the life of God in us due to improper communion, we will not allow death to work in us. Even in the church setting, we will try to save our life by means of self-justification, various devices of the flesh, and walking after our own understanding. We will not allow ourselves to "be defrauded," just as the Corinthians would not suffer that "death." However, neither will we know the life of God that would be released in us if we "loved not our lives unto the death."

There is for us a great feast prepared by God. It is comprised of the "manifold grace of God" that He has deposited in his saints. It is the riches of His glory contained in those who have repented and abide in Him. There is no end to those riches.

8

Appreciation Of The Body Of Christ

I. Effectual Workings

It is impossible for any individual member of the Body of Christ to calculate the contribution made to that member by the other members. We are indebted to so many who have given themselves on our behalf. Some of those who have added to us are quite obvious; others may not be so easily recognized and valued.

At times, I have been asked if I had ever written a book. The first thought that would come to me when so questioned was, "How could I ever get past the acknowledgments?" I knew I could never fully "give credit where credit was due."

Shortly after coming to the Lord in 1970, I began attending Friday night meetings at a Full Gospel church. Usually, only a handful of people attended. The first part of the meeting was spent waiting upon the Lord. No one did anything but sit in silence. I knew nothing about waiting on the Lord, but I did conform to what everyone else was doing. After a period of waiting, some would give testimonies. Then there would be a time of prayer at the altar. On certain occasions, the leaders of the church would pray over us and even prophesy.

When certain things were spoken over me, I thought, "These people do not know me very well." Some of the things seemed so far-fetched that I did not let their words sink down deep in my heart. They were saying such things as, I would be preaching the gospel on foreign lands to many people.

It is easy for me to understand why Sarah laughed when she heard that she was going to have a baby very late in life. It all seemed so ridiculous. The words spoken by these leaders were preposterous to me. I was a person filled with fears and self-awareness. Furthermore, I thought in order to preach the gospel one must be a minister; and to be a minister, one must go to some kind of Bible school. I had no intention of becoming a minister or of going to Bible school. And I was absolutely convinced I would never set foot on foreign lands.

Yet today, those words have been fulfilled in my life. That which was necessary to get from where I was at the time of those meetings to where the prophesies were fulfilled, was supplied by God and often through other members of the Body of Christ.

II. From Here To There

"For ye see your calling, brethren, how that not many wise men after the flesh, not many mighty, not many noble, are called: But God hath chosen the foolish things of the world to confound the wise; and God hath chosen the weak things of the world to confound the things which are mighty; And base things of the world, and things which are despised, hath God chose, yea, and things which are not , to bring to nought things that are . . ." (1 Cor. 1:26-28).

God takes the "are-not's" and makes them the "are's." Where does God get His mighty, His wise, and His noble, but from those very "are-not's" which He calls. And those He calls lack in so many ways. God's call will magnify our weaknesses in our own sight. Gideon is a good example of such vision.

When the call of God came to Gideon, this man went to great lengths to convince the Lord that he was the least qualified individual in all of Israel. In Gideon's own mind and heart, God could not have made a poorer choice. (Sound familiar?) Even after having an angel speak to him, and having God prove himself in two fleeces, Gideon was not able to do God's will. But God is gracious and longsuffering. He comes to Gideon with yet another word to strengthen him and enable him to do the will of God.

"Arise, get thee down unto the host; for I have delivered it into thine hand. But if thou fear to go down, go thou with Phurah thy servant down to the host: And thou shalt hear what they say; and afterward shall thine hands be strengthened to go down unto the host. Then went he down with Phurah his servant unto the outside of the armed men that were in the host" (Jdg. 7:9-11).

"Then went he down!" Why? Because he still feared! How human he was. How encouraging to us! When Gideon obeyed God, God strengthened him with might in the inner man:

"And it was so, when Gideon heard the telling of the dream, and the interpretation thereof, that he worshipped, and returned into the host of Israel, and said, Arise; for the LORD hath delivered into your hand the host of Midian" (Jdg. 7:15).

He, who was the "are not" in his own mind and heart had become the "are." God's call will take us out of ourselves and bring us to places in Him where our heart cries, "This is the Lord's doing and it is marvelous in our eyes!"

III. Occasions Of Grace

We must be careful not to "forsake the assembling of ourselves together" for one never knows what impact a particular meeting may have upon his/her life. For example, one woman in our church was involved in a car accident, leaving her unable to support her head for even a short time. Yet she was faithful to every service, even though she had to rest her chin on the pew in front of her. One Sunday morning, after she had suffered this way for quite a while, the Spirit of God moved in our midst. During a time of tremendous praise and worship, the Lord touched this lady and healed her instantly. No one laid hands on her or prayed for her at that time. But what if she had used her weakness as an excuse not to attend that service?

There have been three services in particular wherein the entire course of my life has been changed. The Word of God is powerful. It can take a man who is going in one direction and turn him completely around. When the Lord saved me, He touched me in a very dramatic way. People recognized the call of God upon my life much more readily than I was willing to admit. For three years after the Lord called me, I continued to work in the business world, but without any inward satisfaction. Attending church services became difficult because it intensified the Lord's witness to me that I was not where I was supposed to be. Nevertheless, our family attended most services including those on Sunday nights.

One of these services was conducted by another teacher from the Bible school that I eventually attended. The minister that night spoke regarding Elijah's message to a rebellious people. "And Elijah came unto all the people, and said, How long halt ye between two opinions? if the LORD be God, follow him: but if Baal, then follow him . . ." (1 Kings 18:2). There were many people in that service, but they all seemed to fade away as this man spoke. It was as if he was holding up a mirror in front of me saying, "Look at yourself." God had gotten my attention. And by His grace, I surrendered to Him that night.

How can we repay such ministers for their faithfulness to God? One thing we can do is to highly appreciate them for the work that God does in us through them. Every time that man's name is mentioned, my heart says, "Blessed is he who came in the name of the Lord." The Word of God was powerful enough to enable me to quit my secular job, sell my house, and take my wife and four children off to the adventure known as Bible school.

So much of God's work is done in secret. Even those closest to us may be completely unaware of what is going on. How much of our potential is hidden behind that which in us is natural. Isaac loved Esau. Therefore, Isaac loved him who God hated (rejected). Isaac had determined to bless Esau in spite of God's rejection of him and in spite of the Word given to Rebecca that the younger (Jacob) would rule. Apparently, Jacob's spirituality and potential were not readily discerned by Isaac, perhaps because Jacob acted "naturally" so often. But God looks upon the heart and sees things that we are unable to see.

We in the Church must be careful not to judge after outward appearances. We must also be careful to allow room for the grace of God to change and enrich others. We cannot put others, as to our opinion of them, at a certain spiritual level or capacity. One of the main functions of the Body of Christ is to increase itself in love. Such increase will show itself in those who entered the kingdom after us. It will show itself even in those that we have ministered to in their need and weakness. It will show itself in their surpassing us in an area or areas of growth. Barnabas went and sought out Saul of Tarsus. Later, in Scripture, Saul's name is changed to Paul, and he is given a ministry that matched and excelled even the original apostles of the Lord.

If we judge after the natural, we will be drawn to what appeals to our carnal man in other people. We must set aside such judgment and approach others in faith, hope, and love, knowing that God is able to make all grace abound toward those we may feel are inferior. God can quickly take one who seems to be last and make them first. Just as God did with Joshua, He is able to do with others: "This day I will begin to magnify thee in the sight of all Israel . . ." (Jsh. 3:7). God is a God of abundance, He pours out His blessings upon us daily in such a way that we cannot contain it all. And He has chosen human instrumentality as a means of imparting his grace to us.

"From whom (Christ) the whole body fitly jointed together and compacted by that which every joint supplieth, according to the effectual working in the measure of every part, maketh increase of the body unto the edifying of itself in love" (Eph. 4:16).

As we "hold the head," we receive the grace and life He would have us minister to the Body. As we contribute, the Body is edified and increased: The more the contributing members, the greater the edification.

True ministry in the Spirit cannot always be measured by apparent results. Since much of God's work is done in secret, we may not know of an effective work in the life of another until long after that work is done and that "which is hidden is made manifest." In some cases, as with Stephen and Saul of Tarsus, the effective work is manifested after the death of the minister of God's grace (in this case,

Stephen). Popularity, numbers, buildings, and other outward "evidences" of success can be very misleading in judging true spiritual worth.

When the "many disciples" forsook Jesus when he gave them words they could not swallow, did his ministry diminish? And when even the eleven scattered when the Lord was crucified and he was left alone, did his ministry cease? We know, of course, that not only did it not diminish, but it increased beyond our ability to comprehend the scope of it. True ministry can only be measured by whether or not that which was done was done in the will of God. Any true judgment concerning such ministry must await the Judgment Seat of Christ at whatever time His judgment may be applied to that ministry. Do not allow your concept of ministry to be restricted by traditional ideas.

Consider the "ministry" given by God to Job — a ministry spoken about by Paul in Ephesians:

"To the intent that now unto the principalities and powers in heavenly places might be known by the church the manifold wisdom of God . . ." (Eph. 3:10).

God called upon Job to "witness" to Satan. "Hast thou considered my servant Job?" What a witness Job rendered. His ministry was in Spirit and power. Job's "ministry" had few outward results, but as to spiritual richness, it was exceptional. Do not measure ministry by apparent results, but rather by the quality of the spirit in which it was rendered. When the Lord comes and judges, He often corrects our previous judgment. He said, "Many that are first will be last and many that are last will be first." Who put many of the first, first? And who puts the many of the first, last?

IV. Spiritual Values

Not all members of the Body of Christ carry a correct appreciation for one another. The Corinthians made the mistake of choosing one minister to the exclusion of others. In so doing, they were shutting themselves off from the supply that might come from those whom they were rejecting.

"Now this I say, that every one of you saith, I am of Paul; and I of Apollos; and I of Cephas; and I of Christ. Is Christ divided . . ." (1 Cor. 1:12-13)?

We become limited expressions to the unlimited fullness of the Lord. Of His grace have we all received. Some are given that grace in certain aspects that others do not receive. Are all apostles? Are all teachers? Do all have gifts of healing? The obvious answer is no. But all have grace to offer in one form or another.

"As every man hath received the gift, even so minister the same one to another, as good stewards of the manifold grace of God" (1 Pet. 4:10).

Diversity in the Body should be cause for unity, not division. What we lack individually is made complete by the Body. We should rejoice that others can supply what we cannot. That God-ordained dependency one of another promotes unity in the Body. One in great need is humble of heart and very open to receive from another. Blessed are the poor in spirit for they are able to receive

> Diversity in the Body should be cause for unity, not division.

of the manifold grace of God that comes to them through many members. But if we think we have it all, we can lightly dismiss even an exceptional member of the body.

Some of the Corinthians did just that to the apostle Paul. Because of their carnality, they could not correctly value this great man of God. Oftentimes we come in contact with a minister of the gospel who has paid a great price to obtain the riches he now possesses in the Spirit. But this minister will not begin to cite any of the sacrifices he/she has made. Because in making these sacrifices, a change has taken place (a humbling) in the man or woman of God that would not allow for such self exaltation. The Lord Himself preached the gospel and never mention what He had to pay in order to carry the anointing. And most did not know or even care that He had to pay a price. Many who received from him did not even bother to show any appreciation, such as nine of the ten lepers. Others who spoke well of him at one time, turned on him at a later time. Paul experienced the same things. At one time, the Galatians were willing to "pluck out their eyes for Paul." But a change took place in them and they rejected him.

"I am become a fool in glorying; ye have compelled me: for I ought to have been commended of you: for in nothing am I behind the very chiefest apostles, though I be nothing" (2 Cor. 12:11).

Paul had to reveal some of the price tag attached to his being an apostle with the hope that it would open the Corinthians to receive him. He did so, not for his sake, but for theirs. He knew that he had much grace for them but they could not receive it because of the hardness of their heart.

Why did he have to become a "fool in glorying?" Because the Corinthians were carnal, and therefore, could not appreciate what he had. They had not paid any kind of price for what they had gotten. Freely they had received from this man named Paul. They were the direct beneficiaries of his ministry without knowing the price he paid so that they could benefit. And their attitude toward him excluded them from receiving yet more.

The first man is of the earth, "earthy." He is a living soul. Therefore, he values all things on that level. The second man is a life-giving spirit. That is a far superior level of living and carries with it a totally different set of values. We in the Church are not to exist on the living soul level. We are to be life-giving spirits. Paul was such. But those on the soulish-realm level did not and could not appreciate that which he possessed.

In order to obtain the values of the "life-giving spirit" realm, one must pay the price in the "living soul realm." Loss must be suffered in the one if gain is to be realized in the other. When one begins to pay the price to obtain spiritual things, he quickly develops appreciation for those who have already paid that price. Abraham was quick to pay tithes to Melchizedek because he recognized the worth of this man. He recognized this man's worth because he, himself, had built altars of sacrifice in his life as well.

How does one place a temporal value on things of eternal worth? Suppose God uses an individual to help restore a failing marriage. Where does the value of that restoration end? For example, subsequent to the restoration, the reunited couple may have more children, who in turn have more children and on and on it goes. None of this would have taken place without the restoration through the minister of God.

In the hymn *Jesus I Come To Thee*, the songwriter pens these words, "Out of the depths of ruin untold, into the arms of the sheltering fold, Jesus I come to thee." If you have been corrected, exhorted, edified, and restored by members of the Body of Christ, and if you have been put on the path of life, you have avoided ruin that you would have otherwise experienced. This is because of the grace of God given through the Body of Christ. How valuable is the avoidance of such ruin?

What value does one place upon an individual who is used by God to bring physical healing to others? What value is a man who can open blind eyes, or cause the lame to walk? What value is a man who can give life-changing truth or bring about reconciliation with God? Who had greater value to Israel than those who could truly say, "Thus saith the Lord?"

V. Enlargement Brings Appreciation

"Not boasting of things without our measure, that is, of other men's labours; but having hope, when your faith is increased, that we shall be enlarged by you according to our rule abundantly . . ." (2 Cor. 10:15).

Paul was looking for spiritual growth in the Corinthians. He knew if that took place, "he would be enlarged by them." That is, they would open their hearts to be filled with appreciation for this man who suffered so many things for them even before they knew him. Paul was a veritable treasure chest and carried these riches with him everywhere he went. He had partaken of the "treasures of the wisdom of God hidden in Christ Jesus."

The Lord told us:

"Give not that which is holy unto the dogs, neither cast ye your pearls before swine, lest they trample them under their feet, and turn again and rend you." (Matt. 7:6).

The swine the Lord mentions here are obviously people who have no appreciation for that which is quite precious to you. The pearls may be an experience with God, a time of intimacy with Him, some secrets He has shared with you, or words of what He will do with you in the future. All these things become our "pearls." But to share them with some one who has no appreciation for such things will result in them casting your words to the ground, and then turning and wounding you with the scornful words that come from a lack of appreciation.

Such lack of appreciation should not exist in the Church. As we dedicate ourselves to the Lord's will for our life, we will incur loss and pass through tribulation. In so doing, we will gain an ever increasing appreciation for those of like precious faith. We will be like children, who after becoming parents themselves, begin to see the sacrifice of their parents out of their love for them. We, too, will see love's sacrifice for us expressed toward us through the Body of Christ. Such vision will fill our hearts with gratitude for the Lord and the grace He has so lavishly spent upon the Church. It will draw us ever closer to one another, and the knitting of the Body will be strengthened even more.

9

The Local Body —
Corinthian Or Antiochian

I. The Longings Of The Spirit

If the Spirit of God is allowed to have His way in individuals in the local assembly, then His purposes will be accomplished and great blessing will result. In order to cooperate with the Spirit, we must know His desires for us. He carries great desires for us as evidenced by the intercession He makes for us that we cannot put into words. The Spirit of God prays the will of God for us in groanings that cannot be uttered, oftentimes contrary to what we would pray.

God hears our heart. One of the members of our congregation, who was going through much tribulation, said, "I never prayed for such dealings." My reply was, "How do you know you did not pray such a prayer, for God hears your heart?"

James, in his writings, attempted to alert the "brethren" to the Spirit's desires for and in them:

"Do ye think that the Scripture saith in vain, The spirit that dwelleth in us lusteth to envy?" (Jas. 4:5)

When writing to this group of believers, James gave similar exhortations

127

and corrections as did Paul when addressing the Corinthians. He admonished these believers concerning their insensitivity to the desires of the Spirit of God. We can be the children of God and still be unaware of His heart toward us. The people in Jeremiah's day did not know God's heart which was so much for them. Therefore, the Lord sent the prophet to tell them:

"For I know the thoughts that I think toward you, saith the LORD, thoughts of peace, and not of evil, to give you an expected end" (Jer. 29:11).

David, on the other hand, was very much aware of the care and desires of God both for and in him. He praised God for the "preciousness" of those thoughts.

Our Lord lived his life on earth with a constant awareness of the Spirit's longings. He expressed these longings with words such as, "Jerusalem, Jerusalem, how oft I would have gathered you under my wing." Being driven into the wilderness to be tempted of the devil, setting his face like a flint toward Jerusalem and the cross, and daily laying down his life were all done by powerful urgings of the Spirit.

Paul, in his epistle to the Romans, speaks of the powerful desires of the Spirit of God.

"For if ye live after the flesh, ye shall die: but if ye through the Spirit do mortify the deeds of the body, ye shall live" (Rom. 8:13).

We see then, that one of the desires of the Spirit is to put to death our carnal nature — and for good reason! The carnal nature is dead toward God and only death can come out from it. So then, the Lord would slay our carnal nature in order to bring us into life. Without the Spirit of God, we are dead in trespasses and sins. We have nothing in us to make us alive unto God and His desires. But when the Spirit of God fills us, He quickens or makes alive our mortal body to express the will of God:

"And if Christ be in you, the body is dead because of sin; but the Spirit is life because of righteousness. But if the Spirit of him that raised up Jesus from the dead dwell in you, he that raised up Christ from the dead shall also quicken your mortal bodies by his Spirit that dwelleth in you" (Rom. 8:10-11).

This quickening of which Paul speaks relates to our doing the will of God in our mortal body. The law could never accomplish such a thing. The law attempted to govern carnality which cannot be subject to the law of God. God then empowers us through His Spirit to do that which we once could not do:

"For when ye were the servants of sin, ye were free from righteousness. What fruit had ye then in those things whereof ye are now ashamed? for the end of those things is death" (Rom. 6:20-21).

II. Union With God

Sin ruled over us. We were powerless to fight it because we are carnal, sold under sin, and our carnal mind could not be subject to the law or desires of God. We were not, nor could we possibly be, one with God. Have you prayed for such a union — yourself to be one with God? If so, that desire and prayer originated in God's will and work in you.

The Lord is bringing all things into subjection to Himself. All things will eventually pass through the Judgment Seat of Christ. That which is one with God will remain. That which is contrary to God will be consumed and God will become all and in all (I Corinthians 15:28).

In order to bring us into union with God, the Lord will bring us to the end of ourselves. We can make "that trip" willingly, reluctantly, or kicking and screaming along the way. "He must increase; I must decrease." That is one of the desires of the Spirit of God in us. For without that desire working, no natural man would choose the path of decrease. Without the aid of the Eternal Spirit, no natural man would lay down various aspects of his temporal life.

There is a decrease that must take place within a certain time period because we have only so many years upon this earth. These years pass quickly and with them opportunities to become all God would have us to become. That is why Paul admonished the Corinthians, "The time is short." If we "redeem the time" and cooperate with the Spirit's desires for us, the decrease will result in increase. However, there is a decrease that takes place out of the timing and will of God that results in eternal loss.

Without a correct heart condition we will have no part in the "all" of God. Daniel was told that when the end was come, he, Daniel, would stand in his lot, or portion, or place in God. That portion belonged to him because he was joined to God by God. When Simon desired to buy the power of God with money, Peter rebuked him:

"But Peter said unto him, Thy money perish with thee, because thou hast thought that the gift of God may be purchased with money. Thou hast neither part nor lot in this matter: for thy heart is not right in the sight of God" (Acts 8:20-21).

Unless our heart is made right we will be excluded from having a portion in the Lord's inheritance. Being aware of God's purposes and longings for us enables us to readily cooperate with His workings. But if we, through hardness of heart, are unaware of what God desires to accomplish, we may hinder or even destroy what He would do in and for us.

Sin hardens our heart and deadens us to the desires of the Spirit. We should be gaining an ever-increasing sensitivity to the Spirit's desires. Obedience increases that sensitivity, as does inward stillness and rest. We are all filled with much unrest and noise inside until God brings us into rest. The noise of many voices and many desires fills our hearts. This noise then allows the enemy to express his desires and thoughts in us without our being aware of the source. James remonstrated with the brethren that their wisdom was not from above. He then pointed out to them who was prompting their words and actions:

"This wisdom descendeth not from above, but is earthly, sensual, devilish" (Jas. 3:15).

Because of their inward unrest, the brethren brought sensual and devilish methods into the Church resulting in division, warring, and death. James equated their sensual and devilish methods to "friendship with the world and enmity with God." All the while these activities were going on, the voice of the Spirit of God was lost in the tumult of sin. James then provided the solution for the problem wherever these conditions exist:

"Submit . . . to God. Resist the devil, . . . Draw nigh to God, . . . Cleanse your hands ye sinners; and purify your hearts, ye double minded. Be afflicted, and mourn, and weep: let your laughter be to mourning, and your joy to heaviness. Humble yourselves in the sight of the Lord, and he shall lift you up" (Jas. 4:7-10).

The Church in Corinth gathered in the same noisy, tumultuous atmosphere as described above, and they, too, were ignorant to the desires of the Spirit. But the Church at Antioch was free from such things and therefore, knew what the Spirit of God desired among and from them. "Separate me Barnabas and Saul for the work whereunto I have called them" (Acts 13:2). We are to bring the "rest of God through faith" into the assembly by our becoming still inwardly under the direction of the Holy Spirit. Just as the Lord drove the moneychangers from the temple in Jerusalem, He would drive the traffickers of this world from His temple of today — the believer.

If we are being reduced to nothing concerning self and being made one with God, our portion in the inheritance of the saints is always increasing. If, by trying to save our life, we resist union with God and live to ourselves, we will have little or no portion of the "all" of God.

III. A Reckoning

"Likewise reckon ye also yourselves to be dead indeed unto sin, but alive unto God through Jesus Christ our Lord" (Rom. 6:11).

It is in our power to "reckon" ourselves to be dead unto sin. We have the power of choice through the enabling of the Spirit. We can respond to people's sins against us by acting out of the old nature. If so, we are at that time, alive unto sin. We frustrate the grace of God, live after the flesh, and produce death. But if we yield to the Spirit, sin does not have dominion over us. We then "sow to the Spirit" and reap eternal life.

This eternal life can be measured by the fruit of the Spirit that has been produced in our lives. The fruit of the Spirit results from the Spirit's Word being planted in us. Then he watches over it, waters and nourishes it until the seed has grown and matured into fruit in our lives. There is an imitation fruit that mimics the fruit of the Spirit, but the imitation fruit cannot feed the Body of Christ.

IV. Abounding Grace—Reigning Grace

"But where sin abounded, grace did much more abound: That as sin hath reigned unto death, even so might grace reign through righteousness unto eternal life by Jesus Christ our Lord" (Rom. 5:20-21).

One day while visiting a certain manufacturing plant, I was introduced to an individual in authority. While driving into the plant, I noticed that the atmosphere was one of hardness. Steel, stones, concrete, and buildings covered the area in a maze of complexity. No trees or plants could be seen to "soften" the environment. Upon being introduced to this man, I quickly found a greater hardness in him than existed even in the plant area.

The man looked at me but did not greet me. When he did begin to speak, his sentences were filled with obscenities. Some of his sentences were only curse words and nothing else. At times he would repeat the same curse word two or three times and say nothing else. While observing his behavior, I wondered what had brought this man to such a wretched heart condition. I only had to endure him for 15 minutes. He had to live with himself for 24 hours a day, every day.

He was a perfect example of the description given of sinful man by Paul in Romans: "Their throat is an open sepulchre; with their tongues they have used deceit; the poison of asps is under their lips: Whose mouth is full of cursing and bitterness . . ." (Rom. 3:13-14).

He never said one pleasant thing during the time that I was with him. His bitterness was not directed toward any one individual. But sin was abounding in him. Yet, as I stood before him, I sensed the grace of God abounding toward him. The thoughts of God were to save this man. He did not know God's thoughts toward him. He was "without Christ, being an alien from the commonwealth of Israel, and a stranger from the covenants of promise, having no hope, and without God in the world . . ." (Eph. 2:12).

The word "alien" means to be a non-participant. This poor creature was unaware of the blessings of God. He had never joined in a Spirit-filled assembly and had his heart overflow with appreciation for the goodness of God. Tears, shouts of joy, praises, and thankfulness never came from his mouth. He was without! – without God, without hope, and without the knowledge of the Spirit's desires toward him.

The Lord longed to open his blind eyes and deaf ears. He longed to take the cursing out of his mouth and fill it instead with blessing. How the Lord longed to fill the emptiness in this miserable heart. He longed to make this man a new creature in Christ Jesus.

"That as sin hath reigned unto death, even so might grace reign through righteousness unto eternal life by Jesus Christ our Lord" (Rom. 5:21).

Paul knew first hand about the grace of God abounding toward a sinner. He, himself, was at one time "a blasphemer and injurious." But the longsuffering of God showed itself toward Saul of Tarsus in the people he persecuted. Their response of the goodness of God to him even while he was persecuting them, became the "pricks which were hard to kick against." Paul tells us that his conversion was a pattern to show the love and longsuffering of God toward sinners. That pattern and expression is to come from God's people. Grace is to reign in them unto eternal life in others.

As we allow the grace of God to rule in our lives, we bring life to any situation. The grace of God cannot be defeated, only rejected. His mercies are new every morning. He would have the Church express those new mercies as well. Do we have enemies? – strong and bitter ones at that? If God's grace could love us while we were yet enemies, then God's grace can love our enemies through us.

From moment-to-moment, and in any given situation, we determine whether grace or sin will rule in our hearts. As saints, we are called to have dominion over sin. If someone sins against us, we are to respond in grace. If we do not, we quench the Spirit of God in us and frustrate His grace. We suffer defeat. The grace of God knows no defeat. While on earth, the Lord was full of grace and truth; He was never defeated.

When sin reigns, it reigns unto death. That is, it destroys relationships with people and with God. The man whose heart and mouth were filled with cursing was the servant of sin. He had no power in himself to rule over it. He would push people away from himself by his self-strength and arrogance and bitterness. Sin repels; grace draws. When grace flows out of an individual, others can taste and see that the Lord is good. When the Pharisees "gnashed upon Stephen with their teeth," they tasted grace. When the Philippian jailer was about to kill himself, the very ones he mistreated gave him grace. Grace reigned in Paul and Silas unto eternal life in the jailer. Grace is to reign in and out from the Church. Eternal life in the church and in others will be the result of such a reign.

V. A "Spirit-Filled Church"

In order for a church to be truly "Spirit-filled," it is necessary that those who attend that gathering yield themselves to God. He gives the Spirit to those who obey Him" (Acts 5:32). The carnal nature of the believers must have been dealt a death blow and be in control of the Spirit. We see this atmosphere in the church at Antioch described in the book of Acts:

"Now there were in the church that was at Antioch certain prophets and teachers; as Barnabas, and Simeon that was called Niger, and Lucius of Cyrene, and Manaen, which had been brought up with Herod the tetrarch, and Saul. As they ministered to the Lord, and fasted, the Holy Ghost said, Separate me Barnabas and Saul for the work whereunto I have called them. And when they had fasted and prayed, and laid their hands on them, they sent them away" (Acts 13:1-3).

What a blessed situation this gathering must have been. When they came together it was for the better and not for the worse. Among the personalities mentioned here are Barnabas, and Saul (Paul). Yet there was no conflict, no division, no one saying, "I am of Apollos," or "I am of Paul." There was no schism in the Body. Why? Because the Lord had the preeminence among them. They were knitly joined together with Christ as the Head in His rightful place in the Body. They had the mind of Christ.

"And he is the head of the body, the church: who is the beginning, the

firstborn from the dead; that in all things he might have the preeminence" (Col. 1:18).

It was not in any of the hearts of the men who gathered at Antioch to rise one above the other. They had, through the Spirit, emptied themselves of ambition, pride, and envy. They did not come to be ministered unto but to minister. They had waited upon the Lord at home, so that when they came together, they were able to feed others the living bread that they themselves had eaten daily. Theirs was a gathering of hearts filled with humility, meekness, longsuffering, and peace. In such gatherings there is indeed a feast.

It is a wonderful thing to experience the move of the Spirit of God in any given service that results in the unity of the Body. To see all those present come down in lowliness of heart and give the Lord the preeminence in their words and attitudes is indeed a little bit of heaven on earth. It is a God-created atmosphere where the Lord is given His proper place in individual hearts.

When Paul wrote his epistles to the different churches, he could always look back to the group at Antioch as an example of what "church" should be. He knew that the only way to create and maintain such an atmosphere is by giving the Lord His rightful place in the Church. That is why Paul always "preached Christ." What did he give the Church at Corinth? Christ! At Philippi? Christ! At Ephesus? At Rome? "We preach Christ and him crucified." Paul was very narrow-minded. But it is good to be narrow-minded when you have the only solution to an existing problem or situation:

"For I determined not to know any thing among you, save Jesus Christ, and him crucified" (1 Cor. 2:2).

In an atmosphere like that of Antioch, the gifts of the Spirit will be in operation. And they will be used for the glory of God and not of man. The members at Antioch were able to speak on God's behalf because they were yielded to the desires of the Spirit. "Separate me Barnabas and Saul!" They knew the mind of the Spirit. Such a separation would cost the local Body at Antioch two very profitable brothers. It would require the members to give financially to support this missionary endeavor. But the Spirit's desires ruled the members who gathered there.

135

Humility, prayer and fasting, giving, hearing, and unity: All of these things were present in the hearts of the believers. And because these things filled their hearts individually, the Church overflowed with the goodness of God, the fruits of righteousness, the unity of the Spirit, and the prosperity of the Lord. Such an atmosphere is not to be the exception, but rather the norm.

VI. Fitly Joined Together

"From whom the whole body fitly joined together and compacted by that which every joint supplieth, according to the effectual working in the measure of every part, maketh increase of the body unto the edifying of itself in love" (Eph. 4:16).

There is to be an effectual working in the measure of every part. Everyone is to be contributing because they have first received. We are to increase in maturity and fruitfulness. We are to increase in our ability to know "the love of Christ which passeth knowledge." The word "passeth" means to exceed or excel. Peter had knowledge that Jesus was the "Christ, the son of the Living God," but at the time of the crucifixion it took him only so far. John the beloved was at the cross because "love exceeds knowledge." Love contains knowledge; it envelops it; it holds knowledge correctly. Love will take us where knowledge cannot.

Paul says we can be brought to a place where we "may be able to comprehend with all saints what is the breadth, and length, and depth, and height; and to know the love of Christ . . . !"(Eph. 3:19-20).

How could we ever be brought to such a place? To "comprehend" is to receive and then express the love of God. God so loved the world He gave His Son. Think of all the repulsive characters contained in the "world" the Lord so loved. This love was extended to all those who were God's enemies, all those who would reject Him, hate Him, even blaspheme Him.

VII. The Secret Of The Lord

"The secret of the LORD is with them that fear him; and he will show

them his covenant" (Ps. 25:14).

The fear of the Lord is a heart condition that holds God in awe. It is an awe resulting from us seeing (to some degree) His glory in comparison to our human frailty: His holiness in comparison to our unrighteousness, His omnipotence in comparison to our weakness. Such a heart attitude will bring us into an intimate relationship with Him. He will share His secrets with us. These secrets become a knowledge enveloped in love. And this knowledge and love will empower us to walk contrary to those who do not have such knowledge. It will enable us to suffer the misjudgments of men. And it will infuse us with strength in the inward man to walk in places that were at one time inaccessible to us.

Isaiah saw the glory of God and he declared:

"He shall see of the travail of his soul, and shall be satisfied: by his knowledge shall my righteous servant justify many; for he shall bear their iniquities" (Isa. 53:11).

By His knowledge! That knowledge was based upon an intimate relationship with His Father. He carried that knowledge daily as he walked the earth. And because of it, he was able to endure the rejection of men while gaining the victory of the cross. His knowledge was obtained on paths of humiliation and decrease. But the decrease resulted in glorious increase.

"I gave my back to the smiters, and my cheeks to them that plucked off the hair: I hid not my face from shame and spitting" (Isa. 50:6).

The verses before verse 6 tell how God awakened the Lord "morning-by-morning" to share His knowledge with Him. When the Son began His daily routine in the carpenter shop, He had already spent much time in intimacy with His Father. It was their relationship that strengthened Him with might in the inner man and enabled him "to bear the iniquity of many."

How many times did someone enter his carpenter shop and yell at him out of their dissatisfaction for the work he had done? How many cursed him, cheated him, or made unreasonable, angry demands? But by his knowledge, out of a love relationship with His Father, He was able to give them grace.

If such knowledge and strength is in the Church, love will rule and cover a multitude of sins. When the Lord began his earthly ministry, the intimacy with his Father continued and increased, thus he was able to bear the increased persecution as well.

The local Body can have what the Church in Antioch had, or it can degenerate to the level of the spiritual atmosphere at Corinth. It can sink even lower than that. God's ways alone will produce true Biblical prosperity in the believer and in the Church. The communion of the saints can grow in ever-increasing richness. If the foundation is Christ, if the Head is Christ, if the Church's wisdom is Christ, if the righteousness is His, then the Church will contain "the treasures of the wisdom of God hidden in Christ Jesus." There will be one faith, one Spirit, one Body, and one Lord. And we will with one mind and one mouth glorify God.

Conclusion

Knowing the truth will set us free. Have you seen that God's work concerning you is to change you in the inner man to conform to His image? If so, you will come into a rest and peace in regard to what others might lack toward you or might do against you. This peace will enable you to avoid being offended by others' imperfections. Such a revelation will free each of us from trying to change everyone else to please ourselves.

Paul tells us we are to "forbear one another in love." All relationships that we desire to deepen will be tested. Our imperfections will put a strain on those relationships. Unless we meet those imperfections with the grace of God, we will fail the test. The result will be a broken relationship or yet another church split. Or we may leave the present local Body, with whom we have gathered, to find something more acceptable to our lack. But in leaving, we will take our imperfections with us and those imperfections will cause future problems in the next group.

Can a given local Body come into that which God would have for it? The church at Antioch is proof that it can. As you have read this book, your heart may have said, "Oh to be joined together in the unity of the Spirit with other Christians!" Do not go out looking for such a group. Rather, turn your eyes upon Jesus. Let the light of life shine into and out of you. Become what you are to become in Him and allow Him to direct you to fellowship with the group He desires. Abide in Him, moment-by-moment and you will meet the needs of others. Abide in Him and their lack toward you will not defeat you. You will bring life to every situation you encounter.

Knitly Joined Together

To read the Word, to mentally agree with it, and even to rejoice in it is not enough. We must heed the admonition given in James 1:22-25:

"But be ye doers of the word, and not hearers only, deceiving your own selves. For if any be a hearer of the word, and not a doer, he is like unto a man beholding his natural face in a glass: For he beholdeth himself, and goeth his way, and straightway forgetteth what manner of man he was. But whoso looketh into the perfect law of liberty, and continueth therein, he being not a forgetful hearer, but a doer of the work, this man shall be blessed in his deed."

We must take the Word and apply it to our lives in our relationships with others. It is the personal application of the Word that causes the blessing to be released. We have looked into the mirror of God's Word and we have seen, to some degree, the glory of the Lord. Truly seeing the glory of the Lord and the light of life will birth a hope in us that we can become pure even as He is pure. This hope will keep us abiding in Him and the blood of Christ will purify us from all sin. Abiding in Him will cause us to become more and more conformed to Him while we behold His glory.

God continually pours out His grace upon us. He is so faithful to us, and we are to be faithful to one another as well. The manner in which God has loved us is to be the manner in which we are to love one another (1 John 4:11).

A Prayer
Lord, we have looked into the mirror of your Word and we have seen both You and ourselves. We desire that You would fill us with Your Spirit so that as You are so would we be in this world. May we be workers together with You by expressing Your heart of love and forgiveness to others. Let us not be forgetful hearers, nor those who forget what manner of man they are, but cause us to ever behold Your face that we may be changed into the same image from glory-unto-glory by Your Spirit. Make us a member of the Body of Christ that functions as You would have us function: Giving and blessing others with that which we have received from Your abundantly giving heart. May Your eternal life abide in our hearts so that others can taste and see that the Lord is good. Knit our hearts together in the love of Christ that there will be but one Lord, one faith, one Spirit, and one Body. Amen.